Wheels Around Sutton
Lichfield and Tamworth

John Bassett

Brewin Books

First published February 1997 by
Brewin Books, Studley, Warwickshire

ISBN 1 85858 090 0

British Library Cataloguing in Publication Data

A Catalogue record for this book is available
from The British Library

Typeset, Printed & Bound in Great Britain
by Heron Press, Kings Norton, Birmingham.

Wheels Around Sutton
Lichfield and Tamworth

Contents

PREFACE

"Wheels around Sutton" is a collection of many individual, written, verbal and photographic contributions, in addition to my own observations and opinions. The contributions are acknowledged through the book, including those by specialists, who have corrected the MS.

In some instances, contributors have not been sure of the source of their information, but we have in good faith., noted the person/s believed to be the initial source.

In conclusion, I would like to express my appreciation to my publisher, Mr Alan Brewin; the main MS reader, Mr Jim Adler; my secretary, Mr Brian Redman, and my ever-tolerant wife, Joan.

John Bassett

Lichfield 1997

Introduction

The motivation to write Wheels Around Sutton emerged during, and after, completing Cross City Connections, Brewin Books, 1990, which had involved seven years' research on Sutton Coldfield's two railway routes, via Four Oaks and Sutton Park. The focus was mainly centred around 1940-1990. At frequent intervals in CCC, comparisons were provided between services and fares supplied to our local populace by the railway network and the Midland Red from its Upper Holland Road operation and A.T. Hastilow's Tudor Rose coaches in Park Road, Sutton Coldfield. When I reflected on the CCC material, the obvious and considerable contrasts appeared of one of the most successful market leaders within the UK of bus and coach operators with the small, strongly independent proud family coaching and removal company. How well, one wondered, was the community of Sutton Coldfield served by these David and Goliath organisations for the 39 years they both operated side-by-side in that part of Warwickshire? Did the giant MR cause problems for its smaller Sutton neighbour? Or perhaps it had major concerns that prevented it from taking a close interest in Tudor Rose coaches? Why were Hastilow's Parade dining rooms so popular with MR crews who had their own subsidised canteens, 5 minutes walk away?

In the 1940's I believed that MR and Hastilows were the two pioneers in bus and coach services in the area. As far as I was aware, Hastilows were the only local removal company. Were there others around? My subsequent research has revealed fascinating facts with many other companies to consider and new questions to be answered? "Wheels Around Sutton" will focus on what the people of Sutton and further afield have shared from their memories and experiences of MR, Hastilows and a number of other significant connecting organisations within and outside Sutton Coldfield. This publication is not a text book on the Midland Red or Hastilows. It is rather a collection of material, much of it previously unpublished., trying to show how such companies fitted into the local community; providing services for generations of Royal Borough residents. However, a number of expert opinions will be used, and given credit, to ensure some technical data is offered, though such knowledge will not be my own!

Chapter One

1860-1920s Transport changes in Sutton Coldfield

Sutton's early transport and removal pioneers.

It was my impression that A.T. Hastilow had pioneered removals and char-a-bancs travel in Sutton Coldfield in the 1920s. However, investigation revealed that in Kelly's "Directory of Warwickshire", the 1880 entries for furniture removals show that the earlier transport and removal pioneers, were: "Allport, WM, of Station Street, Sutton Coldfield", and they had competition in 1880 from Allen Gunnell in the nearby High Street. Bob Allport's leaflet on the early days of the family business quotes 1876, when it was founded at the present Station Street site,, but he advised me, "In our early days we were in business in a small way from Duke Street, moving to Station Street, which afforded good opportunities to transport passengers and goods from the Railway Station" built by the LNWR and opened on 2nd June, 1862. The business thrived and Mr. William Allport "soon operated with some 40 horses". Bob advised me that in the late 1880s his relatives provided horses and Victorian Carriages to take Doctors on their Sutton Coldfield house visits. They also hired horses to travelling sales persons of the time such as the staff at Brooke Bond. Mr Allport recounted how "the traveller from that company went on a week's tour, delivering orders, taking new ones, along a semi-circle route such as Sutton, Coleshill, Leicester, Measham, winding his way back to the Station Street depot". Mr. Allport stressed the need for sales staff in the late nineteenth, early twentieth centuries to be competent in the care and driving of horses, because the travelling salesman was responsible for the hired horse, ensuring it was fed, watered and adequately rested each night it was away from Sutton. Michael Bird gives a potted history of the Sutton Coldfield Fire Brigade in the "Sutton Coldfield Fire Station - 30th Anniversary 1963-1993" which deals with the Sutton Coldfield Volunteer Fire Brigade set up at a public meeting on 21st July, 1886. In those early days "Horses for Brigade use were made available by local tradesmen, who received 15s 0d per horse for their hire. When calls were received, the location of the local tradesman had to be established, a runner sent to them to tell them their horses were needed, so that the Brigade could respond. The situation lasted until 1897, when the provision of horses was taken over by the Highways Committee". This example of horse transport for the benefit of the community operated from the fire station in the Mill Street Town Hall, now the Masonic Hall. The Midland Red Sutton office was in the Masonic Hall in 1926. The Birmingham and Midland Motor Omnibus Company Ltd, was registered on 26th November, 1904. The motor buses made a false start. The Diamond Jubilee booklet of the company, p. 6 tells us, "Breakdowns were so frequent that in 1907 the mechanical vehicles were sold, and for the next four or five years the little red-horse-drawn buses continued to clatter along the Birmingham highways". According to the informative Part One history of the B & MMO Co Ltd, 1904-1933, published jointly in July, 1961, by the PSV Circle and The Omnibus Society, pp 1-2, the distinctive colour of the developing organisation began in 1900. An order was placed by British Electric Traction, part of the earlier BMMO family tree "for new omnibuses with Messrs Birch Bros., of London. It was decided to have them painted red, this being the most conspicuous colour, so the 'Red' of the Midland Red was born".

Proposed tramway system

The Sutton Trades and Labour Council tried to persuade Sutton local authority in 1903 to introduce a further transport system in the Royal Borough. Those proposals remain unknown to most Suttonians in the late 1990s. Fortunately for me, Robert Pritchard [of the Sutton Local History Group] possesses the November 1902 plans for a proposed system of tramways within Sutton Coldfield. The local solicitor, Thos. V. Holbecke, and Sutton engineer, W.A. Clarry, were both involved in the drawing up of the proposals. Former assistant to the Sutton Coldfield Borough Surveyor, Arthur Spencer, informed me, "Early in the 20th Century, Sutton Coldfield Borough Council endeavoured to get a Tramway Bill through Parliament. The routes included : a] Along the present A5127 from the Borough boundary at Erdington to Watford Gap, b] A loop route 'Horse and Jockey' along Jockey Road to 'Park Hotel'. Then along Boldmere Road to join route a] at Chester Road/Sutton Road junction, c] a branch to the Electricity Works and Depot in Riland Road". Arthur added, "None of these were constructed". The plans indicate the town centre to the generating station and depot was routed via the lower parade to Coleshill Street. The Bill was passed as far as the preparation for the Royal Assent. Mr Lyatt, the Managing Director of the City of Birmingham Tramways Co Ltd, wanted permission to continue the lines from their terminus into Sutton Coldfield. The Sutton authority resolved, "time was not ripe for public discussion". The idea of a through line for trams between the city centre and Sutton Parade was still a live issue 9 years later for the Sutton Council General Purposes Committee in 1912. The committee decided, "to take no further steps until a sufficient and satisfactory demand be made by the rate payers of the whole of the Borough for the same". Sutton never had its own tramway system. As far as Mr Spencer could recall neither Tamworth or Lichfield had a tramway system. The wisdom of the time recommended a population of at least 30,000, or two nearby authorities combining to raise that kind of population, to make a tramway system financially viable, and initially attracting the substantial capital needed.

In July, 1904 Mr. O. Cecil Power, Omnibus Manager of the Birmingham and Midland Tramway Joint Committee wrote to the Chief Constable of Warwickshire wishing to extend his omnibus services from the 'Swan' at Erdington "as far as the corner of Park Road, Sutton, or any other terminus you may suggest, if you would kindly grant me permission to do so". Mr Power gave the police official nine days notice before he intended operating the horse-drawn vehicle on sunday, July 31st! He had his eye on Sunday and Bank Holiday runs "but if the route proves remunerative I contemplate running a regular service on week days also". Mr Power showed his persistence in May, 1905, having missed the Sutton Town Clerk, Mr R.A. Reay Nadin "by 2 or 3 minutes" when the Sutton official called. Mr Power, now working for the BMMO Company Ltd, gave an insight into something of the company's North Birmingham operations in its early days. He told Mr Nadin, "At present we are running 2 or 3 horse omnibuses between Salford Bridge, Gravelly Hill and the Swan Hotel, Erdington". He still had in mind a Sunday-only service continuing along the main road to a terminus at the Hotel on the corner of Park Road. The omnibus operator anticipated it "would take several buses and a large number of horses to maintain a regular hourly service on Sundays". In the long term he conceded there "could be pecuniary reasons" to develop a weekday hourly or half-hourly timetable. The stages were:

> Salford Bridge to Station Road 1d
> do. to Swan Hotel 2d
> do. to Chester Road 3d
> do. to Vesey Road, Wylde Green 4d
> do. to Park Road, Sutton 5d

Mr Power expected a good take up on Sundays because of "a very meagre train service". Never being a man to mince his words, he went on to ask for char-a-bancs to be licensed in case there was a need to supplement the omnibuses. The

Sutton Council minutes stated,, "The council resolved not to be entertained"! Tracing the Hastilow 'Family Tree' in 1908, four Hastilows are listed in business; one being Alfred Thomas Hastilow, whose initials were used on the char-a-bancs and removal vehicles in years to come. At the time, he was a butcher in Riland Road,, and his wife, Mrs Elizabeth Hastilow, was a shopkeeper at 8, Parade. According to the Hastilow family, these premises opened in 1903 as a shop with a cafe at the rear of the premises. Miss Ford worked alongside Mrs Elizabeth Hastilow.

The emergence of Chambers

In 1911, the Sutton Borough Hackney Carriages and Fire Brigade Committee issued licences for eighteen horse carriages, twelve motor carriages and thirty drivers' licences. One of the earliest motor bus operators in the Royal Town was Chambers Co. Parade, who in 1912 ran an hourly service from Sutton Parade to the Chester Road Tram Terminus to supplement a restricted train service from 7 a.m. to 10 p.m. The single journey was 5d, 8d for a return and the loading was a maximum of 8 passengers at any one time. The same committee in April, 1912, did not grant Chambers' application to run a motorbus on Sundays, but agreed they could on Good Friday and Bank Holiday Monday as often as required. Chambers was warned not to carry an excess number of passengers. In 1913, C.J. Hastilow, a builder and contractor of Lichfield Road, Four Oaks, was given a one-month licence to use a motor vehicle as a Hackney Carriage. The Midland Branch of the Omnibus Society drew my attention to V.L. Johnson, of Jockey Road, Sutton, who around 1914, ran a Metallurgigue, 20 hp. convertible 14 seat chara/lorry, registration OA 7063. Alan Mills pointed out that this is a "very early example of a French vehicle". The 14-seater was sold in October 1923. What happened to it in WWI? Incidentally, the name 'chars-a-bancs' according to the Editor of the Midland Red Staff

IN PARLIAMENT.
SESSION 1903.

SUTTON COLDFIELD
TRAMWAYS.

Plans and Sections.

(NOVEMBER, 1902)

THOS. V. HOLBECHE.
SUTTON COLDFIELD.
SOLICITOR.

BAKER, LEES & CO.
54, PARLIAMENT STREET,
WESTMINSTER, S.W.
PARLIAMENTARY AGENTS.

W. A. H. CLARRY.
SUTTON COLDFIELD.
W. C. C. HAWTAYNE.
LONDON.
} ENGINEERS

The Title from the little known 1902 plans, loaned by Sutton Coldfield Local History member, Robert Pritchard (Robert Pritchard)

Bulletin, of August, 1954, p.5 "was simply French for 'wagons with benches'," On the removal front, William Allport's son, James William, in 1910, "took over the business which prospered until the outbreak of the Great War in 1914, when most of the horses were commandeered by the Army, and many employees went into Military Service". Just prior to WWI, J. Price of Lower Parade, offered a choice of furniture removing to Allports. With the growing public conversion to motor traction, a year or so before the Great War, in 1913, a fleet of twelve Tilling-Stevens TTA vehicles, operating from the Midland Red garage at Tennant Street, off Broad Street, Birmingham, was used to develop new services including those in an around Sutton. Gray, Keeley and Seale, comment, "All the existing horse bus routes were speedily converted to motor traction, and during 1913, local routes were opened up in Smethwick, Oldbury and Sutton Coldfield. In the last named Borough the Town Council insisted on single-deck vehicles. It was not until 1938 that Midland Red double-deckers were used generally in Sutton Coldfield". With Sutton's Upper Holland Road garage opening on 27th August, 1934, the BMMO' vehicles on the Sutton routes were supplied for the initial 21 years, by Birmingham garages.

It seems the MR decision to standardise on the petrol-electric type of motor omnibus prevented the commandeering of a wholesale takeover of the Red buses for the WWI effort because the War Office believed the Company's choice of vehicle was not suited to war conditions. The War Office decree was probably acceptable to the Midland Reds dynamic executive duo of Traffic Manager, Mr Power, whom we have already noted and Mr. L.G. Wyndham Shire, the Chief Engineer, who had very different approaches to the operation of the BMMO. It was shortly after the motorised MR single deckers were seen around Sutton, that the Borough Surveyor began making demands of the developing omnibus group to stop where the passengers wanted, rather than what suited the company. We can see the continuation of an intriguing, long-running set of circumstances, with Mr. O.C. Power seeking to get the best terms for his company, at the expense of the Sutton Council and the local community. Council officials, however, demonstrated they were not intimidated by the Traffic Manager when four of them, Councillors Taylor, Cartwright, Wareing and Harrison, took the MR to task over safety aspects of the Tilling-Stevens vehicles. The BMMO official acknowledged the local authority's complaint that the front entrance of the bus was dangerous in case of fire. Malcolm Keeley told me : "The War Office disapproved of Tilling-Stevens petrol electric buses because of the transmission system whereby the engine drove through a dynamo and electric traction motor rather than an orthodox gearbox".

At the time of the interview with the council representatives,

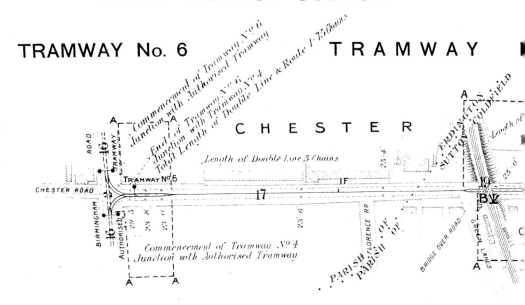

COUNTY C
BOROUGH AND PARIS

ERDINGTON
URBAN DISTRICT COUNCIL

TRAMWAY No. 6   TRAMWAY

The details from these plans show how the Birmingham an

the Company was operating 4 vehicles, sometimes 5, on the Sutton services. Mr. Power promised that a new type of bus being built had an emergency door at the back and the bus had electric lighting. There was discussion over the calibre of those early MR conductors. To attract "a better class of men, remuneration was being increased". At times Mr. Power appears to have had his back against the wall, because the Councillors queried whether the Company needed more than the licences for 6 buses, 6 drivers, and 6 conductors "to enable them" [the BMMO] "to give a more frequent service" to Sutton passengers! Dissatisfaction over the Sunday service on the Boldmere route led to it being discontinued at the Council's request. In answer to Mr Power's protests that the Boldmere services did not pay they again emphasised that an improved timetable could bring the company a better financial return!

Possibility of an early Sutton BMMO garage

There were two other significant issues raised in the Spring, 1914 interview with Mr. Power. The local council seemed unsure who had the authority to allow smoking on the BMMO and Co. vehicles. The Traffic Manager advised the council officials that it was the "Local Authority's responsibility to decide if smoking be allowed" on buses running in their area - not the vehicle operator. Incidentally,

Sutton Council resolved on 13th July, 1914 that "the back part of the new bus be reserved for smokers". It has taken a long time to reverse such a ruling. The Councillors appeared to recognize in raising a further issue with Mr. Power, the advantages of the developing omnibus operators, having a base in the town, with employment opportunities for local people. They asked the Traffic Manager if his company would build a garage in Sutton. He said, "his company would do so at a cost of say £500, if a 3 years licence was granted". He went on to inform the Councillors, the BMMO & Co. "desired facilities for through running to Tamworth, Walsall and hoped to run from Sutton to Birmingham for a fare of 5d or a return fare of 9d". Perhaps the first world war put paid to an early Midland Red bus garage. It was almost another twenty years before the 1934 one, when the Council received £283 for the land, including the additional acreage needed by the BMMO and Co. In November 1914, Sutton passengers complained that Midland Red buses in the town had no service numbers displayed. In early 1915, Mr. Power was again in disagreement with the Sutton Authority. His company, he told them, would not pay for any new licences.

A.T. Hastilow, 1919 temporary licence

Bob Allport brings out a positive point from WWI for Sutton Coldfield, with the Allport employees returning with

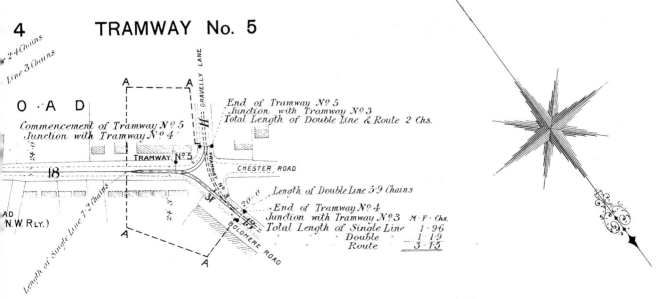

Coldfield Tramways would be connected (Robert Pritchard)

experience and training as skilled motor vehicle drivers and mechanics, which the Sutton firm was able to utilize, as the horse drawn vehicles were replaced by motors for passenger and goods work. In May 1919, the council turned down Allport's application for a Brake, and Mr. F. Hastilow to use a motor lorry as hackney Carriages between the Parade-Chester Road. However, five months later, Hackney Carriage licences were granted (for operation during the rail strike] to Alfred Thomas Hastilow, The Erdington Mechanical Transport Co., and Herbert Taylor of Lichfield Road, Aston. These are the first indications of the Hastilow founder having an interest in public transport. Readers who remember A.T. Hastilow's coaches from Park Road, probably knew them under the name of Tudor Rose coaches and that name was taken into the Harper Bros. fleet in June 1960, when they bought out the Sutton family business. However, it is of interest that the Tudor Rose emblem was approved by the Borough Council to be emblazoned on either side of the Sutton Fire Station appliances in 1920, just over a year before Tudor Rose coach adverts appeared in the Sutton Coldfield News, of Saturday, 16th July, 1921. It is shown on the cover of the Fire Station Anniversary booklet. It is not clear if the 1920 founded Chambers, sole agents for Fords in the town, were the same family that ran the hourly service referred to in 1912. However, according to David P. Howes, the Joint Managing Director, of the expanded company in Coleshill Road, Sutton Coldfield, Mr. Harry Chambers had two apprentices, Frank Arnold; and Mr. George Rose, who

became involved in public transport in Tamworth. Rose Bros., of Central Garage, Tamworth, advertising in the July 9th, 1920 issue of the Lichfield Mercury, told readers they had "the finest and most comfortable" [charabancs] "in the country, having a seating capacity of 28,19,14,9. Reduced fares on Monday, Tuesday, Thursday and Friday, holidays excepted". Another superior charabanc operator in Staffordshire at the time, A.P. Sanders, of the Spot Garage, Chasetown, advertised their Silent Knight vehicles. Sanders apparently took bookings to: cricket matches, race meetings, carnivals, band contests and conveyed works outings. An influential company to make its mark on the Sutton Coldfield transport scene in 1960 as already briefly mentioned, began, according to the Omnibus Society Midland Branch's Honourary Chairman, Alan Mills, in 1922 when Mr. Cecil George Harper started his business with a Model T Ford. Incidentally, A.P. Sanders became part of the Harper Bros, group many years later. Mr. E.J. Eccleshall, the Harper Bros. Traffic Manager from early 1946 until the Midland Red takeover in April, 1974 wrote that "a limited service began between Heath Hayes and Cannock. Cecil George Harper was joined a few years later by his other brothers, Albert Edwin and Victor Edward Harper, with Miss Mary E. Harper, their sister acting as Secretary. The business started in premises in Hednesford Road, Heath Hayes, gradually extending as the company grew". One of the delights and nightmares of local history research is whether to keep to one's original brief, in the case of Wheels Around Sutton; the

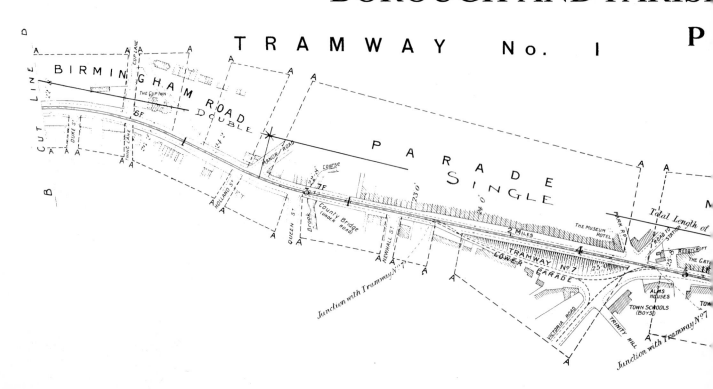

The Course of the main route was along what is now th

Midland Red operations in Sutton Coldfield and the activities of Hastilows Tudor Rose coaches and furniture removals, or as other significant names like Harpers and the West Midland Passenger Transport Executive come on the scene, how much if any prominence do they receive? I shall mention as I have already begun to, large and small operators if it helps to give a wider picture at the time, but the major players will be the Sutton Midland Red, Hastilows and the take over by Harpers, with again the Midland Red, who, themselves, get swallowed up in the end! It is recognised that by briefly introducing an operator it can be an irritant to some readers who for whatever reason, would have liked the author to pursue that lead in greater depth, bringing the story into the late 1990s. Perhaps even the little amount of data given will be sufficient to stimulate the reader to do their own research and offer it to the local studies department of their Area library. The other main task for me is to make "Wheels Around Sutton", as mentioned earlier, a non technical, but interesting resume of people's memories and experiences as they made and were involved in the creating of history in the local communities of Birmingham, Sutton Coldfield, Lichfield, Tamworth.

Midland Red and Walsall Corporation Services

Continuing with one of the major foci, the Midland Red and Lichfield, the Mercury recorded in 1920 that the omnibus company "is now running daily services between Lichfield, Rugeley and Stafford". The first service leaving Lichfield at 9.15 a.m. The Mercury also advised local travellers of the 4 buses each way by the same group connecting their city with Sutton and Birmingham. The Midland Red in a 1920 Sutton News advert appeared to look down on football supporters when it stated "Saloon Motor Buses can be booked at any time for private parties of any description - Horse Char-A-Bancs for football matches"! A growing list of Sutton Council concerns in 1920 resulted in a sub-committee, chaired by the Mayor, being set up to discuss them with representatives of the BMMB Co., The six subjects were : a] Problems on the Walmley and Oscott routes, b] Standing at Chester Road corner, c] Distinguishing marks on buses, d] Arrangements for queues, e] Shelter accommodation, f] Stopping places at Manor Road, Jockey Hill, and the corner of Florence Road and Chester Road.

Perhaps learning from the BMMO Co's potentially unproductive methods of negotiations with the Sutton Council, the Walsall Corporation's approach to the local authority about its route into Sutton in 1920, appeared to be more conciliatory when they spoke of "suggesting a conference to fix the termination of their contemplated route". The new omnibus operator in the area soon received the local authority's blessing to introduce the service. Mr. Power having got wind of the competitor, modified a Red route from Streetly Lane to Walsall Road. The council minutes imply the alteration had already been made! Mr. Power was "requested that the Streetly Lane service be

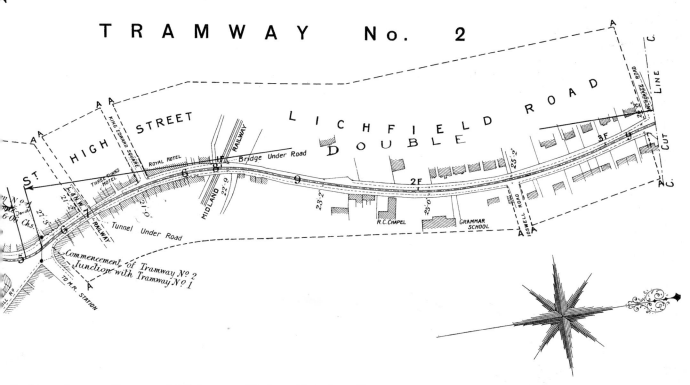

...cluding the gradient up Mill Street. (Robert Pritchard)

resumed". The Traffic Manager of the Midland Red in the winter of 1920, re-emphasised his earlier concern over the two operators running services along the same route from Streetly; the Midland Bus inevitably running at a loss. Reflecting on the first nine months of 1920, Mr. Power complained that no Bus or Railway Company "was making any profit today owing to petrol and wages". At that time, each new bus cost the Red £2,000. The only Sutton area service that paid was from "Birmingham to Mere Green. The Walmley route cost a shilling per mile, average fares taken were 8d per mile." The Red Traffic Manager decided "the New Oscott route must be abandoned and the Walmley one reduced to 2 buses a day". Mr. Power, arguing from a poor set of financial results, could not afford to pay shelter rental, though he was willing to reconsider the issue a year later. The Sutton Mayor did not believe Mr. Power's hard-up story. He thought "the figures were no good without an audit". In January, 1921, W. Mills of 278 Highbridge Road, Wylde Green, registered OH 2698, a model Ford, that could be either a van or a 14 seat bus.

A.T. Hastilow and Son garage opened

Presumably, neither of the Midland Red duo were pleased to hear that 'Sutton's first luxury Coach and Removals garage' had the foundations laid in Park Road for Mr. A.T. Hastilow, in February 1921. Jackson and Insley were the Builders from Elms Road, Sutton. The purpose of the garage was for "motor storage and general commercial use". The completed garage was inspected and passed as satisfactory on the 28th June, 1921. There is some mystery, however, where Hastilow's staff gained their previous experience, claiming to be "packers with 25 years experience with careful drivers". This claim was made in 1921. F.H. Vinyard of 19, Mason

An early example of a Midland Red operated Tilling Stevens Vehicle, CH1232, near Mold, North Wales in around 1925 on a Birmingham - Llandudno Service. (Mr Davies. Senior)

Road, Erdington in 1939, claimed 30 years' experience in the removal business. Hastilows also offered motor engineering in all its Branches. The Park Road people further claimed to be running six first-class Motor Coaches to Stratford Mop on October 12th, 1921, leaving the Parade at 9.30 a.m. Five were already booked. Existing records from the Omnibus Society reveal A.T. Hastilow only owned one 26-seater chara at the time. Where did the other five come from? One from W. Mills? Yet another Hastilow claim in the autumn of 1921 was, "We are the pioneers of Motor Coach trips in Sutton and consequently know best how to cater for the public". Seats could be booked at Hastilow's Dining Rooms, Parade, Sutton Coldfield, and the Garage, Park Road. There is a feeling from Hastilow's public relations in the press that they had been around well before the Park Road garage was built. Anyway, the company offered Motor Coaches complete with the most up to date lighting systems. The first 'Tudor Rose' advert appears to be in July, 1921, and refers to 'The Queen of Motor Coaches', presumably the Daimler CK, AC 9984 that seated 26 passengers. The evidence unearthed suggests A.T. Hastilows were not the pioneer Chara or Coach operator in Sutton, though an early force to contend with by other independent operators and as Hastilows grew, even by the mighty Midland Red. It is not clear if the 1914 registered V.L. Johnson was related to or the same as the Johnson Motor Co. of Duke Street, Sutton, who ran in 1921 a fourteen seater Crossley light Motor Coach with pneumatic tyres to Rhyl, Colwyn Bay and Llandudno. There seemed to be a choice of either a day trip or staying a week. Johnsons promised to collect patrons' luggage free at 8.30 a.m., the coach departing at 9.30 a.m. Further competition for A.T. Hastilow came from an unnamed company located at 1 Highbridge Road, Wylde Green [the same road as W. Mills] who hired out 2 or 3 ton lorries, and available anytime for furniture removals.

Harpers American Vehicle

As the 1920s went on, Harper Bros at Heath Hayes, also operated a Chevrolet [USA] 14 seater. Further services Mr. Eccleshall informed me "were operated between Cannock and Heath Hayes [Tuesdays and Saturdays] with an additional service between Heath Hayes and Brownhills to Shire Oak [Saturdays only]. There was also a daily hourly service between Cannock and Aldridge". Now that the beginnings of the Midland Red, Hastilows, and Harpers, the three main reasons for Wheels around Sutton have been identified, we move from a somewhat haphazard approach, to looking, in turn, at the Midland Red Sutton services; A.T. Hastilow's Tudor Rose and removal operations; then further notes on the expanding firm of Harper Bros. At times it will be necessary to highlight connections between the three companies, but readers are less likely to feel travel sick, flitting from one operator to the next. However, some interesting items about Hastilows coach and removal activities from one of their old ledgers will be revealed, showing the involvement of Broads Travel Bureau, a further local, well established business. First, however, we consider the Midland Red services in the Sutton area.

Chapter Two

Sutton's major omnibus operator

Readers who want more detailed background to the then growing Midland Red should consult the excellent two volume work, mentioned before, by Messrs, Gray, Keeley and Seale, published as Midland Red, volume one, A History of the Company and its vehicles up to 1940 and volume two, A History of the Company and its vehicles from 1940 to 1970, Publisher Transport Publishing Company, Glossop, 1978 and kindly loaned to me by Mrs Audrey Kelsul. Malcolm Keeley has kindly given permission for extracts from the two volumes to be quoted in Wheels around Sutton. The other major source, already noted, is the two part work on The BMMO Co. Ltd, jointly published by the P.S.V. Circle and The Omnibus Society. Part one in July 1961, and part two in June 1959. The main contributor to both parts was the late Peter Hardy, for some time a Sutton Coldfield resident. This book re-emphasizes earlier points and deals more with the human experiences of bus and coach operators rather than a focus on technical data. The Sutton Borough and Mr. O.C. Power saga continued in the 1920s with the Traffic Manager telling the local authority officials instead of the quarterly £200 licence charge, the red would pay a once for all concluding fee of £250. He was promptly told the £200 per quarter charge "must be adhered to". One wonders if his bullyboy tactics paid off with other Midland authorities. Mr. Keeley argues that Sutton Council were the bullyboys! In Mr. Keeley's view, Mr. Power was shrewdly managing the Company's financial affairs. Yet about the same time, Mr. Andrews asked "to be allowed to run a motor charabanc during the coal crisis, between Sutton and Birmingham, owing to a shortage of trains", but the council asked "the Motor Bus Co to augment their services" which they did with "extra buses during the curtailed railway service".

No resident Sutton MR conductor/ess

Again, remembering that the Red buses that ran on the Sutton Coldfield routes were from Birmingham garage/s between 1913-1934, not one conductor/ess who received a licence from the Borough for some while, resided in the town but came from Tamworth, Stafford and mainly Birmingham. As may be anticipated there was a predominance of women conductors during, and for some time after, WWI. In 1923, a few years after deciding the Walmley service only warranted two a day, the 'MMOC agreed to additional buses to Walmley on Saturdays'. Presumably this was to satisfy a growing demand from a sudden rise in population after the Great War. In that year the Bus Company provided an alternative service to Birmingham via New Oscott and Perry Barr, subject to agreement over the fares. The Police Superintendent in Sutton spoke of his anxiety "over stopping places on the road near Maney Hill Road". He recommended a compulsory stop outside "The New Hall", near Maney Church. It was agreed by the Council the following month. In 1925, the town's first of its 3 railway stations was closed under the 1923 formed LMS. Sutton Town, renamed from Sutton Coldfield in 1924, opened by the Midland Railway in 1879 in Midland Drive. Sutton Town is the name given in the 1902 Sutton Coldfield Tramway Plans! [see CCC pages 58-60] In the year of the Great Strike the "BMMOC licensed 35 buses, 5 charabancs and licences for Drivers and Conductors all renewed on the same terms as 1925". The power and perseverance of the Borough Council led to the Red decision to "reduce fares between the Parade and Mere Green from 2½d to 2d". Mrs Elsie Turner recollected "alighting from Midland Red buses in South Parade. With all the passengers off, the conductor put a scotch under the rear wheel. He stayed with the bus". According to Malcolm Keeley, the use of the scotch was still used with ex-BMMO stock, half a century later at Stourbridge. 1928 was the first year that no horse drawn carriage had been licensed in Sutton. The relocation of the stopping place for through buses in the centre of the Parade "has considerably reduced the congestion outside the Museum", the Sutton Council were informed.

Review of Midland Red Sutton Services 1913-1928

With the help of Peter Hale of the Omnibus Society, we briefly review the BMMO's first fifteen years operating services in the Sutton area, remembering that the vehicles were all supplied from garages outside the Royal Borough. "The first service started on 10th May, 1913, and ran between Chester Road Tram Terminus and Sutton Coldfield via Wylde Green. This was joined on 16th August, by another service between Chester Road and Sutton, via Boldmere. On 10th October , 1913 these routes were numbered 11 and 12 respectively; it was extended to Mere Green in March, 1914. Services 11 and 12 were renumbered several times over the following two years. The first route to Birmingham was service 18, which seems to have started on 12th September, 1914, and apparently ran through from Birmingham via Sutton to Shenstone. This was soon [later in 1914?] extended to Lichfield as service 18C, and new service 18B, Birmingham-Sutton-Tamworth, also started around the same time. Streetly was first served by a diversion of service 18 to there instead of Shenstone, and Walmley was first served by service 18F, Chester Road-Walmley- Sutton. Unfortunately I do not have starting dates for either of these". Perhaps readers may be able to help me out on these details. "The Birmingham-New Oscott-Sutton route, service 18G, started on 9th August, 1923. A Sundays-only service 114, between Great Barr and Sutton, started in 1927. I

NOTICE.

Extract from Bye-law.

1. (1) Every person who intends to construct a buing to which the foregoing byelaws relate shall give to ie Council notice in writing of his intention and shall sed or deliver the notice to the Clerk or Surveyor of the Cancil together with a sufficient description in writing o:

(2) He shall also send or deliver to the Clerk or Surveyor a plan of each floor and sections of each storey, floor and roof of the building, drawn in a clear and intelligible manner on suitable and durable materials, to a scale of not less than *one inch* to every *eight feet*:

(3) He shall show upon the plans and sections the following particulars :-

(a) the position, form and dimensions of the foundations, walls, floors, roofs, chimneys and the several parts of the building, in such detail and to such extent as may be necessary to show that the building complies with any of the foregoing byelaws which apply to it ;

(b) the form and dimensions of any water closet, earth closet, privy, fixed ashpit, or cesspool to be constructed in connection with the building ;

(c) the level of the site of the building, the level of the lowest floor of the building and the level of any street adjoining the curtilage of the building in relation to one another and above some known datum.

(4) He shall also send or deliver to the Clerk or Surveyor a block plan of the building, drawn in a clear and intelligible manner on suitable and durable material to a scale not less than *one inch* to every *forty-four feet*, and showing :-

(a) the size and position of the building and, so far as may be necessary to show compliance with any of the foregoing byelaws which apply to the building, of the appurtenances of the properties immediately adjoining the building ;

(b) the position and width of any street adjoining the curtilage of the building, so far as may be necessary to show compliance with any of the foregoing byelaws which apply to the building ;

(c) the size and position of any yard or open space belonging to the building ;

(d) the position of any water-closet, earth closet or privy and of any fixed ashpit, cesspool and well in connection with the building ;

(e) the lines of drainage of the building, and the size, depth and inclination of each drain and the means to be provided for the ventilation of the drains ;

(f) the position and level of the outfall of the drains and the position of any sewer with which the drainage is intended to be connected.

If any deviation is needed from the deposited plan either during the course of erection or after completion a plan, showing the intended alterations must be submitted to the Borough Surveyor for his approval before such deviation or alteration is made.

PLAN No. *6328*

BUILDING NOTICE.

Borough of
Sutton Coldfield.

(Please endorse).

For erecting *Motor Omnibus Garage and Offices*

in *Upper Holland Rd. Sutton Coldfield*

for M *Messrs. B'hm. + Mid. Motor Omnibus Co. Ld.*

of *547 Bearwood Rd. B'ham*

From Mr. *Arthur Ashton F.R.I.B.A.*

of *33 Parade*

Leamington Spa

Date *July 11th 1933*

It was a real encouragement during the research into Sutton's major omnibus operator, to be shown this Building Notice and attached plans, located by the Sutton Coldfield Local Studies Staff. (Sutton Coldfield Local Studies Department) Although the Office name for the stream at the side of the upper Holland Road garage is given (item, 13 on the Building Notice), it was known locally as the 'Ebrook'.

(This Notice must be filled up and endorsed, and delivered to the <u>Borough Surveyor</u> with the deposited plans at least Seven Days before the Meeting of the Committee).

July 11th 19**3**

To the Health and Buildings Committee of the Borough of Sutton Coldfield.

I hereby deposit plans for the erection of certain buildings in

Upper Holland Rd. for M*essrs B'ham & Midland Motor, Omnibus Co. Ld.*

of *Bearwood Rd. Birmingham* in accordance with the following description :—

1. Purpose for which the buildings are intended to be used		*Motor Omnibus garage & Offices*
2. Width of Street in front of buildings		*40 feet*
3. Distance of intended line of frontage from Street		*15 feet*
4. Level of lowest floor with reference to Street		*12" average above Street level.*
5. Materials for walls		*brickwork, corr. sheeting on steel framing*
6. Materials for roofs		*Corr. sheeting, asbestos slates, patent glazing*
7. Thickness of external and party walls		*18", 14", 9".*
8. Number of storeys		*one*
9. Height of rooms on each floor		*garage 16'-6" floor to roof trusses. Lean-to b/ps av. about 11'-0"*
10. Area of Site		*not yet known to Architect*
11. Means of Water Supply		*S. Staffs. main in Street*
12. Size and inclination of Drains		*6" & 4" incl. not less than 1 in 48*
13. Description of outlet (*Sewer or Cesspool*).		*Sewer in Rd. S.W.D. in Rd. S.W. to Plants Brook*

I further hold myself responsible for the work being carried out according to the Bye-laws and plans deposited herewith, and for the proper notices sent in during the course of erection.

(*Signed*) *Arthur Ashton Architect*

Postal Address *33 Parade Leamington Spa*

(State whether Owner, Agent, Architect, or Builder).

(P.T.O.)

believe that West Bromwich Corporation's route to Sutton started when Midland Red gave it up a few years later". Malcolm Keeley informed me that "the WBC Service started on 30th July, 1932". " Midland Red Services were Renumbered twice in the nineteen-twenties as its network expanded on 16th May, 1925 and on 11th February, 1928. The Sutton area routes were numbered as follows. [Some of the numbers are, of course, still in use today] : 100 Birmingham-Sutton-Mere Green; 101 Birmingham-Sutton-Streetly; 102 Chester Road-Boldmere- Sutton; 103 Chester Road-Boldmere-Sutton-Mere Green; 104 Birmingham-Sutton-

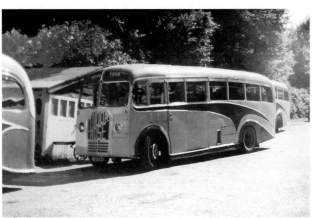

Three coaches of the Tudor Rose fleet on a fishing trip to Holt Fleet in 1947. (K. A. F. Brewin)

Streetly-Cannock; 105 Birmingham-Walmley- Sutton; 106 Chester Road-Walmley-Sutton; 107 Birmingham-New Oscott-Sutton; 109 Chester Road-Sutton; 110 Birmingham-Sutton-Tamworth; 112 Birmingham-Sutton-Lichfield-Burton; 113 Birmingham-Chester Road-Hardwick Arms; and 119 Great

Barr- Sutton".

MR and LMS cajole commercial travellers

Commercial travellers in the Midlands were encouraged in January 1929, to prepare for the "great Spring 'push' and use Midland Red services to achieve a record year of sales". These otherwise non-mobile, and perhaps former Allports clients, would be able to get "to any towns and villages in the Midlands without much trouble or loss of time by using Midland Red, One Day Anywhere, tickets for 5/-, travelling by "any bus and changing vehicles or routes as often as desired". But was there a catch? "Anywhere tickets" it concluded, "are not available on Express Service Buses". However, such Daily Express Service fares from Birmingham to amongst other places were : single 3/6 and 5/- return to Leicester; 2/3 single and 3/11 return to Worcester and 4/6 and 7/3 respectively to Northampton. The LMS had issued a 12/- return to London and a late morning, New Street to Bristol for 5/- including a visit to Fry's chocolate works at Somerdale. It may have been an economic measure brought on by more bus services that forced the LMS in May, 1929 not to replace Mr. H. Larkin at Sutton Park station when he left for promotion to Water Orton, but brought the former Midland Railway station under Mr. G.E. Howlett at the former London and North Western and larger property in Station Street. A railway staff morale booster in the Borough was the Railwaymen's Annual Flower Show, Sports and Gala opened in 1929 by the then Mayor, Councillor W.T. Lawrence who distributed the prizes, including the Silver Challenge Cup to R.J. Robbins of Sutton. The site for the show was the field belonging to Mr. William Fowler and was

Many Suttonians still refer to the pub, next to MacDonalds as The Dog in Sutton, shown in the C1950 view of 1936 built BHA824, a BMMO, SOS Type Fedd, on a 107 Service. (Gordon .B.Davies).

situated adjacent to Four Oaks Railway station. 1929 timetables advertised seven free Midland Red lectures with lantern slides, "complete with descriptive readings on the following topics : 1] Winsome Worcestershire; 2] Famous Homes and Historic Haunts; 3] Leafy Warwickshire; 4] Beauty Spots of the Midlands; 5] Some Midland Rivers; 6] Tours by Midland Red; and 7] Shakespeare's Country". All the places were accessible by the company's services. Arrangements made for soloist and pianist "if required".

Sutton MR services in 1929

The November 4th, 1929 Midland Red Motor Services Official Timetable, one of many, kindly loaned me by Ross Hamilton, list the Sutton area routes under those in the Birmingham, Dudley and Stourbridge Districts. So in 1929 Sutton remained an appendage to Birmingham operations. The listed services were X99, Birmingham and Nottingham via Sutton and Tamworth Express Service; 100 and 101, Birmingham, Sutton, Mere Green; and Streetly; 102 and 103, Chester Road, Boldmere, Sutton and Mere Green; 104, Birmingham and Cannock via Sutton; 105 and 106 Chester Road, Walmley and Sutton; 107, Birmingham and Sutton [via New Oscott]; 110, Birmingham, Tamworth via Sutton; 112, Birmingham, Lichfield, Burton-on-Trent via Sutton; and the 113, Birmingham and Chester Road. The 114 Great Barr [Scott Arms] and Sutton, was suspended for the winter months; and Service 170 Sutton and Coleshill via Minworth and Water Orton was temporarily suspended. The return fare from Birmingham Station Street via Sutton to Nottingham

was 7/6; single from Station Street/New Street all routes to Sutton 8d; return 1/2. The first Birmingham service from Sutton Parade was a 107 at 6.15 a.m. due to arrive in Station Street at 6.56 a.m. The first main road to Birmingham left the Parade at 7.38 a.m., though that seems very late. Advertisers at the time were : F.V. Hartill, Drug and Photographic Stores in Lichfield Road, Four Oaks; Chris. C. Moore, Ironmongery & Household Goods, 10 Boldmere Road; W.H. Nichols, Avenue Stores, Park Road - "Have you forgotten anything for your picnic?"; The Royal Sutton Watch & Clock Depot, 4 Mill Street; Madame Eugenie, High Class Milliner, 84 The Parade; H. Young, The Handy Stores, New Oscott - "I give 6d in the £ discount on all groceries"; Dees & Co., House Cleaning, 77 Parade; and Lloyd, Confectioner, Minster Cafe and Tea Gardens, Market Square, Lichfield. 1929 was the year Alf Coleman began his 45 years service with the Midland Red, beginning in Bearwood for about six weeks training as a driver from his Sutton home. He moved to the Digbeth garage, later to be the long-distance coach station. He told me "As a coach driver we were on the same rate of pay as the bus drivers, but got good tips!"

"The coaches were almost like a charabanc with canvas clips on the roof and a flat radiator. Some coaches picked up at Sutton, Six Ways Erdington and on to Digbeth. Others went to Walsall via Perry Barr". Mr. Coleman spoke with affection of some of the SOS [Shires Own Specification] vehicles, all single deckers until four years after the Upper Holland Road garage opened. The reason that the Sutton Council prevented the Midland Red., Walsall and later West Bromwich Corporation from operating double deckers in the

Parked next to the Sutton Garage Enquiry Office, around 1950, is AHA 513, an updated BMMO SOS Type 'Con' of 1934, seating 38 passengers. (Gordon . B . Davies).

FHA 249 with updated Body is at the Stafford stand in the former Lichfield Bus Station, with a number of old properties, to the rear of the BMMO SOS Type FEDD of 1939. (Gordon . B . Davies).

Royal Town according to Alf was "they assumed passengers would look through bedroom windows. The local passengers protested to Inspector Tucker [the resident inspector at Sutton] about the non-use of double decker buses".

Council versus MR and WCT DDs in Sutton

All the major books on the BMMO. Co. speak of the single decker policy including 'A History of the Midland Red', by R.C. Anderson, David & Charles 1984, p. 49. "Early in the 1930s the BMMO fleet passed the 1,000 mark, and in 1931 additional garage space to accommodate these was provided at Evesham, Redditch, Swadlincote and Sutton Coldfield, the latter known as the 'posh' or 'snob' garage in 1934". On p. 11 "the town council insisted single-deck vehicles only, and it was not until 1938 that double- deckers were used generally in Sutton Coldfield". The double decker issue surfaced again in 1931, with the Walsall Corporation arguing "such vehicles were necessary in the later part of Sundays because servant girls required considerable accommodation". Presumably the girls came from the Walsall working class areas employed in affluent households in Little Aston, Streetly, Four Oaks and Sutton Coldfield, bringing at least a week's clothing etc., with them. After many conferences between Sutton Council and Walsall Corporation officials it was agreed with the Manager of the Walsall Tramway Department "that subject to The Traffic Commissioner's

approval the whole of the Sutton Service, with the exception of Sunday evenings, would be operated by single-deck motor omnibuses". Further exceptions when double-deck buses would run occurred with exceptional traffic loads on Bank Holidays, Annual Horse Show and occasional parties in the summer. In April 1932, West Bromwich Corporation were permitted by the Sutton Council to run "buses on Saturdays, Sundays and Bank Holidays, with the promise that only single-deck vehicles were used. Parking was available opposite the Victoria Road Boys School". Later that year the BMMO was given sole use of a new omnibus shelter in front of the Town girls' school, costing £49.10.0d. "The Bus Company paid 10% per annum of the estimated £60 outlay. All cleaning, lighting maintenance etc., undertaken by Corporation". Mr. Power turned down the Council's request that the Omnibus Company should erect further bus shelters at Lichfield Road [near Railway Bridge], Four Oaks Station [Streathers], Birmingham Road at "Broadfields", Chester Road [Beggar's Bush], Jockey Road and Boldmere Road corner and Walmley Village. However, he considered that Mere Green was sufficiently important for his company to make some financial contribution towards it. Thinking of what other authorities may construe if he agreed to Sutton's needs he wrote, "I am afraid the other proposals that were suggested would create a precedent and would lead to requests at many hundreds of places within the very wide area we cover". Going with my mother shopping at Walsall market in post WWII days, we used to catch the

Pre-War SLR Coach CHA 983 at Sutton, with its updated 1937 Body, is shown at Sutton Coldfield Garage, C1950. (Gordon . B . Davies)

Walsall Corporation buses with wooden slatted seats from the Victoria Road terminus by the iron railings outside the Boys's School where I was a pupil. Malcolm assumed the slatted seats were a wartime austerity. The West Bromwich terminus was in South Parade by Chambers Motors.

MR Upper Holland Road garage

Alf Coleman's journey to work was drastically cut from 26th August, 1934 with the opening of the Upper Holland Road Garage in Sutton. Bob and Doris Hemming recall that the site "was a water-logged site, full of bulrushes. We called it the ousish. [The Swamp]. They had to pile drive it more than once. It took a long time. Up to the opening of the garage the buses came from Bearwood to start their shift, from Sutton". Messrs Gray, Keeley and Seale wrote of the new garage on pp 171-172 "The structure was plainer than earlier BMMO garages although of conventional steel framed, red brick construction. The four bay frontage included some ornamental brickwork, less 'decorative' but neat in appearance. Brickbuilt offices and workshops were included on the site. The original capacity was for 60 vehicles although within ten years this figure proved to be quite inadequate". "Sutton's vehicles were initially a mixture of various single-decker types but by late-thirties no less than 36 'FEDD' double-deckers were in evidence from various batches, including at least 24 of the original HA 94 XX - series". The remainder of the synopsis is on page 172 of Volume Two. The Sutton News advert of Saturday 25th August, 1934 advised readers the garage was to be opened on Monday, 27th August, 1934. The 1st of September News told readers "Saloon coaches and buses could be hired from the new Sutton Garage". David Jenkins said when the "garage opened in 1934, the Resident Inspector was F.A. Kerrison whose title was changed to Garage Traffic Superintendent in 1936. He retired in May, 1954 after 42 years service"

The Sutton paper bus

Alf Coleman sometimes worked the Sutton area paper bus. "It was an early morning start at Sutton Garage, leaving at 3.45 a.m. The driver and conductor wore dust coats. We took the single decker into Station Street, Birmingham, collecting the papers from W.H. Smith. We then dropped off the papers at Six Ways, Erdington, another drop in Erdington village, Chester Road, Boldmere, then Beggars Bush, Smiths of Sutton and on to Mere Green Roundabout. After a hangback at Mere Green with our dust coats off, we took the 8.30 a.m. service to Birmingham, forming the 112, the first of the day, to Burton at 9.00 a.m. from the city. They left Burton after a twenty minute break arriving at Sutton Parade for 11.00 a.m. There was no relief with few drivers at the time". From the management perspective, David Jenkins said, "paper buses operated to reduce the import of any strike action by the main transport vehicle drivers. Quite a number were operated. One from a number of garages - Birmingham, Malvern. Drivers and Conductors", David concluded, "were paid 10 hours each per day". Driver Coleman spoke with pride and satisfaction of the times he sang in the Midland Red choir. He was "only one of two drivers in the choir , the rest were office and management staff. Many such concerts were given in Sutton Town Hall". Sutton Highways Committee were concerned over the footpath outside the new Sutton garage. The footpath was reconstructed in 1934 with alterations in the fall of the carriageway, the cost of the footpath being met by the Omnibus Company. The General Purposes Committee gave the Midland Red permission to store 15,000 gallons of petrol at the Holland Road garage in the summer of 1934. However, the Parks and Estates Committee refused an application for a party of 150-200 persons to be driven through the park in motor coaches!

Double decker debate rumbles on

By the summer of 1934, compromise is being considered on the non double-decker policy in Sutton, perhaps Councillors were receiving complaints on this issue from their voters! A council Sub-Committee had had an interview "with the Manager of the BMMOC with respect to the proposed double deck service from New Oscott to the Parade when certain modified proposals were considered". The outcome still resulted in single deck vehicles only being run by the Midland "Red" in Sutton until 1938. The 2d Midland "Red" and Railways Joint Motor Services timetable of September 30th 1935 lists Service No. 172 running on Sundays only from the Parade at 2.30 p.m. and 8.30 to Coventry via Walmley [Fox Inn], Minworth, Water Orton, Coleshill [Coach Hotel], Stonebridge, and Meriden, taking one hour nineteen minutes for the journey with booked connections to Marston Green, Kenilworth and Leamington. The Coventry [Pool Meadow] services left at the same time, taking one minute less. Two overall fare stages operated. The Parade to the Coach Hotel was 9d, and from there to Coventry, again a single fare, at 1/6. Peter Hale informed me "The 172 started on 20th May, 1934, running only on Sundays". It was in 1935 that Bob Allport as the Chairman of the Allport Company

Alf Coleman in his white Midland Red driver's Coat, at Tewkesbury. This photograph, taken pre-war, shows the advanced full front design of the BMMO "SLR" coach as originally built. (A. Coleman)

sold the 9 taxis to Judges, concentrating on the commercial vehicle side of the business. Walsall double - decker buses came under the spotlight of the Sutton General Purposes Committee in 1936. Complaints had been received from residents on the main roads in the Borough "as to uses of double-deck omnibuses by the Walsall Corporation". Investigation identified that of the 179 per week trips on the Walsall-Sutton route, only 19 had double-deckers, operated to meet special demands. Probably a number were to accommodate the servant girls and park visitors. It was noted the Traffic Commissioners licence authorised Walsall to operate single or double deck vehicles.

Sutton Park station treble training functions

A little recalled fact is the LMS Motor driving school which was set up at Sutton Park station in 1936. In post World War II years, the location became unique in railway history for a small country station, simultaneously hosting a 'railway motor driving school, a training establishment for freight guards and shunters in 1959, and in 1961, a school to train signalmen and women. The LMS continued to offer strong competition to the Red for large group party travel, as shown by the moving of 3,000 Bywater & Co Ltd staff/families from Kings Norton to Sutton Park station, on three special trains on the occasion of the company's annual outing, in August, 1937. In the same month, a new well established retailer, opened at 113, The Parade, building on its success in Nechells, Walmley and Boldmere. John Frost MPS, Chemist, provided a pharmacy that end of the Parade. My wife, Joan, reminded me of a service to the community by another of the chemists that continue to trade in the town, Boots. The Nottingham based group's founder accepted his wife's suggestion to include a subscription library service in some of the Boots branches, including the Boots shop opposite South Parade and the Empress Cinema. Joan, who worked in the Sutton Boots in the late 1950s to the early 1960s, remembers being a staff member of the library. One of the commercial aspects for the venture was that carers stocking up with medications and various accessories for a patient, relative or neighbour took library books for them and themselves, particularly when public library services were not so well developed. The Local Studies and Reference Sections of Sutton Coldfield Library on the former Empress Cinema site informed me that the title of the Boots service was the Boots Cash Chemist Booklovers Library which began in 1900 and ceased operation in 1966. We are not sure how long that private library branch was operated in Sutton.

In 1937, Midland Red bus stops on the Parade were fixed for the following 3 routes 1] The New Oscott service [disembarking only] opposite Longmores shop 2] Walmley Bus opposite Haynes shop and 3] Nottingham bus opposite Fosters [clothiers] shop. The 3 stops were about 30 yards apart. The January-May 1938 timetable had two maps. The whole MR and Railway Joint Motor Services area and the MR termini in New Street was the place for services to: Canwell, Coleshill, Four Oaks, Lichfield, Burton, Mere Green, New Oscott, Streetly and Sutton. Station Street was the departure points for Tamworth and Derby.

Chapter Three

The Midland Red at War

Sutton bus station demand and WWII services

1938 saw the demand for an Omnibus Centre in Sutton. However, towards the close of the year, the Borough Surveyor said "in his view such a centre was not necessary in Sutton due to most services being through services and few terminated in the town". Early in 1939 the Omnibus Centre "was deferred until the proposals relative to the Parade by-pass are completed". The bus station was never built. Bus driving was a reserved occupation in WWII. Because of the limited frequency of bus services Alf Coleman spoke of a 9 a.m Birmingham service, from a pool of 7 buses, with 2 or more buses for each of three services that day. The Midland Red stopped its own vehicle building in the war. A considerable number of Red buses were commandeered at the time of the fall of France, some of which never returned - according to Peter Hardy. Against a background of fuel rationing; cancellation of about 200 services; drastic reduction in frequency of the remaining 700 or so; all long distance services, including the Birmingham to London service were suspended in May 1941. These schedules were noted by Mr. Hardy; the Chief Engineer Mr. L.G. Wyndham Shire, retired in April, 1940. He, with Mr. O.C. Power had made significant contributions to the progress of the BMMO Coy. Mr. Donald M. Sinclair from the Northern General Transport Co. Ltd, took Mr. Shire's job.

National Emergency timetables

Peter Hale noted that the National Emergency timetables were introduced on 24th September, 1939, with temporary suspension of services. As far as the Midland Red was concerned on that date Mr. Keeley informed me, "There was not a shortage of vehicles on 24.9.39. The rationing was to save resources for the war effort and the commandeering of vehicles took place in 1940". At the time "The Midland Red was not too badly off for vehicles, it was able to use coaches on bus services and obtained a number of wartime austerity double-deckers". The local suspended services in the June 1940 timetable were X12, Birmingham-Derby; 172, Sutton-Coventry; S61, Sutton- Wishaw; and S62/3, Sutton-Chester Road. The Sunday services that were suspended were : S68, Erdington [Six Ways]-New Oscott- Sutton-Ashfurlong Corner; and S78, Kingstanding-Erdington- Walmley. However, a 10 minute interval service was maintained on the 107 route for 6 hours on Saturday afternoons. 6/- was the Workman's Weekly return between Birmingham and Sutton; a scholars daily return was 7d, with a Workman's Sunday return at 1/-. A fascinating service noted by Ross Hamilton, was the X15 linking Wolverhampton [Queens Square] and Whitehouse Common [Balloon Barrage Centre] A single ticket costing 1/8d. Alf Coleman thought the BB Centre protected military

establishments in the area and the munition sites on the Sutton side of Birmingham. Alf recalls a smoke screen was created day and night to hide the balloons from enemy aircraft. He did not remember an aircraft tangling with the balloons. With less buses the Red asked private coach operators in early 1941 if they could "let us have any of your coaches on hire at any time of day or on Saturdays and Sundays to help us out with Munition Workers Services, Military and Evacuation Jobs etc.,?" One of the Scholar specials that remained in the 1941 fares table was between Streetly [Parson & Clerk] and the Boldmere Schools. it was 2d return for a child between the Parson & Clerk and Boldmere schools. In 1941 passengers were charged a minimum of 6d from Birmingham up to the Chester Road Tram Terminus and The Fox at Walmley, and 7d to the terminus at Sutton Parade on services 105/6. The Inward-to-Birmingham fare policy was 6d from Harman Road/Erdington Six Ways. A number of services gave guidelines on "Through Bookings - Walmley District; passengers for Walmley district may travel on this service between Birmingham and Chester Road Tram Terminus in either direction transferring there to or from service S65/6".

British Restaurant in Wesley Hall

Just across the Ebrook, 7 years before the South entrance and extension of 1950 was built on the Sutton garage, the inaugural ceremony was held in the Wesley Hall to open the British Restaurant, by Mayor Cllr W. Moss in February, 1943. Seating 200, "The Borough Restaurant" could serve 500 lunches, plus 700 school children lunches prepared in the kitchen. It had been estimated that up to that time, only 5% of Sutton's 42,000 population could be catered for in its catering establishments at lunchtime.

Death of Mr. O.C. Power, Mr. D.M. Sinclair new GM

With the death of Mr. O.C. Power, in October, 1943, Mr. D.M. Sinclair became the General Manager of the BMMO & Company. The joint PSV Circle/Omnibus Society's part one history says on pp 14-15 that Mr. Power "has rightly been described as a breezy and delightful personality, with a character of singular force and originality". Similarly, Mr. Wyndham Shire "was a man of great initiative, original thinking and courageous convictions, and their partnership over the years undoubtedly contributed greatly to the success of the undertaking". The 1941 and 1944 Midland Red and Railways Joint Motor Services Timetable give the Snow Hill and New Street trains, including those on the two Sutton lines to Lichfield, Burton and Derby, and Walsall. Before giving a selection of the Sutton train times, Peter Hardy on page 13 of the joint publication gives some explanation to the Railways involvement with the Midland Red. "In 1928",

This 1962 record of DHA648, a former SOS SD, on tree lopping duties in Reddicap Heath Road, is an example of BMMO vehicles being adapted for other than passenger conveying. (Gordon . B . Davies).

he writes, "the Railway Companies obtained, by Act of Parliament, powers enabling them to operate motor omnibuses; and they decided, rather than to institute probably fierce and wasteful competition with the established road passenger transport undertakings, to establish a financial interest in a large majority of the existing major omnibus companies, including Midland Red". Half of the ordinary B.M.M.O. shares were purchased by the LMS and GWR.

Local rail and bus services in 1944

In the June 1944 Red Timetable, there were New Street departing trains calling at Sutton Coldfield on the former LNWR route at : A.M. 6.25; 7.50; 8.50; P.M. 12.10; 12.25 SX; 12.42 SO; 1.6; 2.15; 4.18 SO; 4.45 SX; 5.15; 5.35; 6.0; 6.45; 7.23; 9.30; 10.52.

The alternative former Midland Railway line gave 5 trains from New Street to Penns, Sutton Park, and Streetly at : A.M. 7.18; 8.13; P.M. 1.10; 5.35; and 6.35 on their way to Walsall. The following bus services were offered in Sutton and district on D-Day, Tuesday, 6th June, 1944 : 4, X99s each way, with 9, 110s to Tamworth and 11, 110s ex Tamworth to Birmingham; 3 pre- breakfast S62/3 services either way including 6.55 a.m. from the Parade to Fort Dunlop, with hourly frequency from lunchtime to early evening; S65 and S66 ran from 7.5 a.m. - 9.5 p.m. to Chester Road Tram Terminus and 8.33 a.m. - 8.40 p.m. to the Parade. The S67 and S76 operated hourly for twelve hours of the day; whilst the S70 ran at two hourly intervals from 10.21 a.m. to

Ashfurlong Corner, and the last service for Sutton left at 6.40 p.m., 7.10 p.m. on Wednesdays. S73 provided 3 pre-breakfast services and hourly runs between noon and 8.15 p.m.; the 100,101,102 and 103 offered a regular interval service both ways from 6.52 a.m. Mere Green to New Street and 6.41 a.m. to the Mere Green [Barley Mow] from the Parade and 7.30 a.m. out of the city. The 104 Cannocks ran three each way at four hour intervals, except on Wednesday with an additional 7.16 p.m. Sutton-Cannock; in contrast with 4, 105/6 buses to Sutton Parade, 6 went to Birmingham. The 37 minute journey 107 Oscotts'. had a 10 minute frequency at times to and from New Street or Bull Street, with Sutton's first departure at 5.23 a.m; 3 services ran both ways on Service 112 via the Parade, Shenstone [Bull's Head], Lichfield [Market], Alrewas [George and Dragon] to Burton-on-Trent [New Street Park] . The 113s had a 45 minute interval operation during the day, with evening services using the Grey's, Bull Street terminus. At that point in the war, Sunday services were still suspended on the S62/63; S65/66; S67/76; and S73. Comparing the 1929 and 1944 X99 timetables it was 5 minutes quicker in the war between Birmingham and Nottingham, with the four Birmingham City Centre departures leaving at the same weekday times of 8.20 a.m.; 11.20 a.m.; 2.20 p.m. and 5.20 p.m. The 1944, 112 services reached their destinations in four minutes less, and had been reduced to 3 services each way.

8 DAYS TOUR OF
TORQUAY AND SOUTH DEVON

5/-
Deposit Secures

TOTAL FARE £6.6.0
AUGUST WEEK £6.12.6

Includes all Travel, Meals and Hotel Accommodation

EVERY SATURDAY THROUGHOUT THE SEASON.   **FULL ACCOMMODATION AND FOUR TOURS.**

Good value in the early '30's - extracts from Broad's leaflets of that period. (Broads Travel, Collection)

Sutton News spills wartime 'beans'

In Part II of Peter Hardy's combined MR history he wrote that in 1945 "it was about that time that a new system of type numbering was introduced. Single deckers S, double deckers D, and later, coaches C". The Sutton News of the 12th May, 1945, reporting after the war against Germany had been won, was released on what information it could print when the Defence of the Realm Regulations were lifted. Readers were told "since 3rd September, 1939, thousands of men and women have passed through the Balloon Barrage Depot. Towards the end of 1942, the United States Army Base Post Office in Sutton Coldfield was set up at Sutton Park station, and a defined area in Sutton Park was used for testing armoured fighting vehicles. A Civil Defence camp had been established near Powell's Pool". A further revelation in Sutton's contribution towards winning the war was the "first testing ground for amphibious tanks was situated at the old brickyard pool in Barnard Road". The MR advert in the News of the 19th May, said "Thank you Forces. The management and staff of BMMO Company Ltd offer thanks and admiration to all members of the Armed Forces who brought victory to the West". With a deserved self pat on their backs the Red management advert continued, "They are proud that during these long years of war, they have been able to contribute their little bit towards 'keeping the flag flying' at home and will continue to do so until the job is finished". The BMMO Diamond Jubilee booklet gave the fleet at the end of the second world war as 1,427 with 6,727 employees.

Chapter Four

Meeting Post World War II public transport demands

Later in May, 1945 the BMMO reported in the media "we thank those who have already made enquiries" about Seaside and Long-Distance Services. The company waited for the all-clear from the Ministry of War Transport to restart, but "neither have we the necessary staff available at present ... Immediately we are able to arrange for any coach services to be resumed" they would give the widest possible publicity. Sunday, 8th July saw the reinstatement of additional X99 services from Birmingham Station Street at 8.20 a.m. and 1120 a.m., via Sutton and Tamworth.

Sutton MR services halted

Less than two months after the war was over a Midland Red event happened that has become forgotten through the mists of time. The introduction of new time schedules, which included late night services and Sunday morning buses, caused a strike at Dudley garage. Sutton employees who came out in sympathy, spoke against the new working day of 13-15 hours. Many travellers to Sutton Park who found there were no bus services, complained to the BMMO and small children had to walk more than two miles to reach school. A rather novel sight was heard and seen on Sunday, 15th July, when a Midland Red strike spokesman toured some of the Royal Borough streets with a car roof sited loudspeaker, expressing his colleagues willingness "to go back to work as soon as the company was prepared to negotiate". He apologised for the inconvenience they had caused the public. Tudor Rose coaches ran some excursions that day! A positive gesture to the hard-done-by MR passengers was the introduction of day services from Birmingham locations. Bookings began at the end of July. Towards the middle of August the workmen's weekly return tickets were discontinued, though workmen's daily return tickets were available for forward journeys up to 9 a.m. One wonders if safety aspects or more vehicles had become available or some other reasons that brought about the early 1946 ruling from the MOWD, Midland Region, for BMMO to reduce standing passengers from 12 to 8 on stage coach services. Malcolm comments, "I suspect the MOWD felt the war was over so emergency regs that allowed 12 standing were withdrawn ... Getting the vehicles for the post-war travel boom, let alone meeting the relaxed regs would take to about 1950 ... Hundreds of buses were delivered in 1946-9, but relatively little could be scrapped". Some readers may have other insights in the the MOWD ruling of 1946!

WBTD service reinstated

Four days before Victory Day celebrations on Thursday, 6th June. the County Borough of West Bromwich Transport Department reintroduced the route to Sutton Coldfield with 8 return services, Monday-Saturday, and 5 either way on Sundays. The 40 minute journey ran between Victoria Road, Sutton and Dartmouth Square in the Black Country town. Presumably the Sutton Town Council was pleased with the 25 service starting again, however they received no satisfaction from the Midland Red who when pressed by the councillors to provide a Sutton-Minworth bus service, were advised they were "unable to institute any new services". Like many public transport employers, the Midland Red garage was desperately short of bus crews, leading to an appeal "Help us to give you better services by providing accommodation for additional staff. Accommodation urgently required at the Midland Red garage, at Upper Holland Road, Sutton Coldfield". The company's shortage of vehicles in early 1947 was accepted by the Regional Transport Commissioner when he approved their application to operate the whole of the Walmley services via "The Anvil". At the same time the BMMO proposed to improve the Boldmere services, including via Boldmere Road, direct to Sutton and another via Gravelly Lane. 1947 and 1948 remained difficult times for recruiting Midland Red staff and accommodating them, but the company provided additional services on many Sutton routes, with some being extended such as the 102 to the junction of Clarence Road and White Farm Road. The service extension coincided with the day the Council closed the sutton British Restaurant, with local caterers offering a dinner for 1/9d.

Fosset's Circus visit Holland Road playing fields

A few hundred yards from the Upper Holland Road garage on Monday and Tuesday 21st and 22nd April, 1947, Fosset's Franco-British Circus and Zoo drew crowds to the Holland Road Playing Fields, with seats priced from 1/6d to 4/6d. In those early days after WWII, such localised live entertainment, new to many children, was a real attraction, without the competition of the television. I assisted some of the animal handlers at the Holland Road site, when different circus shows came. The group of local lads were rewarded with complimentary circus show seats and opportunities to care for a variety of animals town children had never actually seen, apart from in old school textbooks. I was not impressed with the handling of the animals by a number of the circus staff I witnessed in those early post war years, nor having to listen to their foul language. Realistically, it was not an easy life for the circus folk, being in a town for a couple of days, then taking the Big Top down, only to erect it some miles away next morning. Many of the staff had numerous tasks to perform, including ring work before an audience. It was also in April of 1947 that 3 additional Sunday trips each way began on the 113 service, Birmingham-Hardwick Arms. In June, the General Manager, D.M. Sinclair had notice No. 3029 sent to all company staff,

The old and new in Victoria Road, Sutton in June 1960. Wartime Walsall Guy Arab Fleet No.59, with No.844 a Dennis Lolines recently introduced on Walsall Services. (M. Gottschalk).

pointing out the need to recapture the prewar "enviable reputation in the eyes of the public for courtesy, efficiency and punctuality". The G.M. told his staff that any who did not want to attain those standards "would be better to find another job now". It was also in the summer of 1947 that most of the company's employees had the guaranteed week reduced from 48 hours to 44 hours, without loss of pay, with overtime payable after 44 hours worked. A number of other changes of service occurred in the Arbitration Award.

New MR bus trip for Sutton Mayor

The Mayor of Sutton Coldfield, Councillor Mrs Kate M. Garrard with other West Midland invited dignitaries, sampled a new type of Midland Red bus she travelled on to Tenbury Wells on Tuesday, 2nd September, 1947. The mayor declared that it was "By far the most comfortable bus she had every travelled in, as well as being the most attractive),!" She anticipated that the 500 underbody engined vehicles, with a top speed of 60 mph full laden, "should help to ease the transport situation". Just over two weeks later the company asked Factory managements under the Powerless Day Scheme"to advise us immediately if your factory hours are to be altered and Saturday working will be necessary". The managers were warned "your works service cannot be altered at a moment's notice". Alan Mills recalled that there had been a "severe winter in 1946/47 with considerable amounts of snow still visible in March and April, followed by massive floods". Severe power cuts were necessary from the stretched coal power stations throughout the land. So in an effort to stagger the limited power services, a planned availability of energy was forecast to industrial and domestic users.

The Courtesy Campaign inaugurated in 1946, using the motto "There's always time for Courtesy", had "been distinctly encouraging". Mr. Sinclair, looking back after a year of the Campaign, told the staff: "Today, whilst the position has not yet been reversed, it is certainly progressing that way. Complaints are fewer, and compliments are greater in numbers ... Complimentary letters are now coming in at the rate of 20 a week, Sutton conductor, W. Care was mentioned by a passenger who wrote "I have lately seen your notice regarding courtesy and feel that undoubtedly this is the type of person you would wish to recognise". Mr Care was appointed as Traffic Inspector at Sutton in May, 1948. He had a son, daughter and son-in-law at the local depot. A Sutton conductress was complimented in a letter. "I am sure I speak for all the mothers, especially of the smaller children, when I say how much we appreciate this conductress, M. Ryan ..." we would like to see more like her". David Jenkins remarked, "We had two Ryan sisters, both Ms, Margaret and Mary, transferred from Leicester MR".

MR innovations

The October 1947 Staff Information Bulletin gave a review of the company's first coach cruises season after the war. "Though ... we have been able to operate only a modest programme, the cruises have been successful ... We are hoping to put on a bigger programme next year". The autumn of 1947 saw the publication of the ABC of Midland Red Vehicles at 2/6d published by Ian Allen Ltd, and available at BMMO Co Enquiry Offices. Two new Sutton bus services began on Monday, 19th January, 1948. The S60 ran via Lichfield Road, Four Oaks Road, Streetly Lane, Thornhill Road, Sutton Oak Road, George Frederick Road, Bannersgate Road and the Birmingham Road from 7.15 a.m. at two hourly intervals until 9.55 p.m. to Sutton via Streetly, with similar frequency from 8.15 a.m. to 8.55 p.m. via Boldmere. The other new local MR route, noted in January, was the S68 Sutton-Ashfurlong Corner via Tamworth Road, offering six services at two hourly intervals from Sutton at 10.35 a.m. to 8.35 p.m. Mr Jenkins advised me "All new single deck services were operated by Driver Horton and Conductor Sid Smith. Conductor Smith was well past his 70th birthday when he retired". The 113 was revised and additional services offered. A further improved route via Sutton, was the X99/100 providing a 30 minute service, Monday-Saturday from Birmingham at 7.20 a.m. - 10.20 p.m. to Tamworth. From 2nd February, 1948, Midland Red patrons could book for long distance and seaside services, though not more than 4 tickets being issued to any one person. David Jenkins, one of our main Sutton Red contributors joined the local garage in 1947 as a conductor. "Mr. F.A. Kerrison, who began when the Sutton garage opened in 1934 as Resident Inspector, continued in his 1936 designation of Garage Traffic Superintendent, with the Engineering Section under the control of Mr. F. Bacchus".

MR staff hostel in Sutton

An important Midland Red policy decision to recruit sufficient Bus crews came to fruition on 31st January, 1948. The Sutton Coldfield News reported "A staff hostel to accommodate 30 employees of the Midland Red Bus Company has been opened in premises in Vesey Road. The full residential facilities included provision of meals and a lounge. There is a resident Housekeeper/Manager in charge. It is proposed to cultivate land there to provide fresh veg/fruit for busmens' meals. The first BMMO Co hostel was opened at Leamington". David Jenkins told me "Mr. Mrs. Mayne were in charge to November, 1948, with Mr. Mrs. Scott taking over up to the hostel's closure. The first 6 resident men came from Newcastle in the north east, then mainly from Scotland, but 5 came from Malta". David spoke of problems that the hostel staff had to contend with. "Some of the residents caused a lot of difficulties. A number of men", he added, "were trouble makers". It seems that not many of the Scottish staff stayed more than a few months, whilst the Maltese "used it as a means of starting a life in this country and cheap living until established, with meals and laundry facilities provided". Perhaps, part of the staff shortage problem was revealed in the first annual accident record of the 28 garages, at the tail of the list, "remained Wellington, Bearwood and Sutton" in 28th position. Malcolm was aware "The Birmingham area garages always did badly on the accident record, no doubt due to traffic conditions". He could not explain why Wellington had done so poorly. Mr. Jenkins stated, "Extra staff were recruited at Ludlow garage [opened 1st January 1951] to work at Sutton. They were ferried to Sutton daily, being paid from Ludlow to Ludlow for a 14/15 hour day. Lichfield [opened 17th September, 1954] and Tamworth [opened 3rd August, 1928] also provided some staff". However, Sutton's staff hostel opened at the end of January, 1948.

Sutton BMMO services in 1948

On the 7th February, the services in and through Sutton noted by Peter Hale of the Omnibus Society were : X99

Sutton Park played host to many visiting vehicles like EHA 594 an AEC Regal belonging to Nash Ltd. of Smethwick, on a 1962 visit. (M . Gottschalk)

Immediately after the war, the pent up demand for holidays and travel was released. The photograph shows Weston-Super-Mare in 1947, a popular destination for Midland coach operators. The impressive Harrington bodied Leylands of the Gliderways fleet are flanked by a new Guy Arab owned by Allenways of Birmingham. (K. A. F. Brewin)

Birmingham- Sutton-Tamworth-Nottingham; S62 Chester Road-Monmouth Drive; S63 Chester Road-Boldmere-Sutton; S65 Chester Road-Walmley- Sutton; S67 Chester Road-Goosemoor Lane-New Oscott; S69 Chester Road-Sutton; S70 Chester Road-Sutton-Ashfurlong Corner; S71 Erdington-Walmley-Ashfurlong Corner; S72 Sutton- Walmley-Minworth; S73 Chester Road-New Oscott-Parson & Clerk; S76 Chester Road-Court Lane-New Oscott; 100 Birmingham-Sutton- Mere Green [New Inns]; 101 Birmingham-Sutton-Streetly; 102 Birmingham-Sutton-Mere Green [Clarence Road]; 103 Birmingham- Sutton-Canwell; 104 Birmingham-Sutton-Brownhills-Cannock; 105 Birmingham-Chester Road-Walmley-Sutton; 107 Birmingham-New Oscott-Sutton; 108 Birmingham-Erdington-Sutton; 109 Birmingham-New Oscott-Boldmere; 110 Birmingham-Sutton- Tamworth; 112 Birmingham-Sutton-Lichfield-Burton; 113 Birmingham-New Oscott-Hardwicke Arms. There were more Sutton Area service revisions in March, 1948 including : 101, 11 p.m. journey Streetly to Sutton, extended to Chester Road, where it returned to Sutton at 11.24 p.m.; the S72 had an additional Saturday morning service from the town at 9.40 a.m., leaving Minworth at 10.05 a.m. Like other operators the Midland Red had a 12½ per cent fuel cut on tours and excursions and private hire imposed by the Ministry of Transport in the Spring of 1948. The Sutton garage's engineering section experienced a number of changes in the late 1940s when Mr. Bacchus "was transferred to other duties due to ill health in July, 1948, though he admirably impersonated Father Christmas at the annual children's party the next January, attended by over 200 children. Mr. Bacchus's vacancy was filled by Mr. W. Lowe in February, 1949, then by Mr. T. Hobbs until December that year, after which Mr. N.L. Cole remained in charge until May, 1964".

'Pats on the back', followed by 'kicks in the pants'

David recalled that "Ticket issuing machines were introduced at Sutton in August, 1948. The first type was a disaster. The company had to purchase the patent from the manufacturers to get out of the contract. The machines worked well but were open to abuse". The Staff Bulletin started a contrasting feature to "Pats on the back", in August, 1948, "Kicks in the pants" first list included two complaints on the Mere Green services. "One went 5 minutes early, the other because of staff stopping for a smoke and chat arrived 6 minutes late at Canwell". Saturday, 2nd October, "was a significant date when the X12 Birmingham-Sutton-Lichfield-Burton-Derby express was reinstated at 8 a.m., 2 p.m. and 6 p.m. from Birmingham". There was an hourly 112 service from 8 a.m.-9 p.m. leaving Birmingham, a similar Sunday service from 10 a.m., and 3, 104 services each way. The GM asked his staff for reports of small operators who pirated MR timetables by picking up in front of BMMO vehicles, and causing wasteful competition as outlined in the Road Traffic Act of 1930. Mr. Keeley pointed out that "'pirate' operations were not possible after 1930". The GM seemed to know otherwise!

Thomas' Street Guide of the Royal Town for 1948, gives the following two local authority services that ran to Sutton. Walsall Corporation's service No. 6 ran from that town at mainly hourly intervals from 6.55 a.m. - 9.45 p.m. with extras at peak times. Sutton's first service left at 7.50 a.m. at the last at 10.55 p.m. Walsall's first No. 6 departure for the forty minute journey to Sutton on Sundays left at 10.45 a.m., and Sutton's last departure was at the weekday time of 10.55 p.m. According to the 1948 guide, Suttonians had eight weekday No. 25 services run by the West Bromwich Corporation, between 8.45 a.m. and 10.15 p.m. from South

Parade. Similar to the No. 6 route, forty minutes were allowed for the journey. The 2nd June, 1945 WBC service appeared to be the same in 1948.

Miss C.M. Tucker in the Sutton Enquiry Office was considered by a customer "to live up to your slogan 'There's always time for Courtesy'. It would make the housewife's lot much easier if the majority of staff serving in the shops had the sense of proportion of this person!" A passenger in the Sutton area wrote "Realising that I could not reach the stop in time, I turned back and resigned myself to walk. The driver must have noticed my action for when the bus reached me a few seconds afterwards, he stopped the vehicle and I was able to board it after all. Such courtesy and thoughtfulness is rarely found in these days, and I appreciate most sincerely the action of your driver, particularly as the walk was mostly uphill". Mr. R.J. Casey was the helpful driver. It was about this time in the Autumn of 1948 that the Sutton Coldfield Midland Red Sports Club had "been successful in obtaining the leasehold of a piece of ground near the Garage, and they hope to go forward with plans for the erection of Club Premises". Although I am not giving a ball by ball account of the new vehicles put in service by the Red, it is significant to record from the Staff Bulletin of November, 1948, "we have now received a total of 200 post-war buses made up as follows: 100 Single deck [S. 6] type, with underfloor engines. 50 Double deck [AD2] type on A.E.C. chassis. 50 Single deck 'S. 8' type, built to the new width of 8 feet, also with underfloor engines. It is expected that delivery of new single deckers will continue at the rate of 2 or 3 per week, and if the body-builders keep their promise, we should be able also to start putting the remaining 50 'AD 2' type double deckers on order, into service early in the new year"

Leopard spots superseded

The April 1949 Staff Bulletin informed employees that the "Leopard Spots" garage identification system had been superceded by two code letters for each garage on post-war destination blinds. Sutton Coldfield being SN; Birmingham [Bearwood], BD; Birmingham [Digbeth] DH; and Tamworth TH amongst the thirty garages at the time. The June Bulletin recorded the introduction of a new service, the S61 running between Erdington Six Ways and the Tower Estate Sutton. Malcolm Keeley commented that "The coach fleet was somewhat small until quantity deliveries of new coaches for the 1949 season." The October Bulletin spoke of a "very important increase in frequency granted on a trunk route viz. between Birmingham and Burton-on-Trent. Before the war, this service was operated every two hours but last autumn was increased to operate every hour. One winter's experience proved that even this frequency was insufficient and in April, 1949 we applied for a half hour service. This time we were opposed by the Railways and although we made efforts to reach agreement ... the application had to be fought out in court),. The service was increased to every thirty minutes on service 112 from 5th November, 1949. The Company continued to see an increase of interest by the younger generation in its vehicles. From the start of issuing complimentary Fleet Reference Books in May, 1946 up to December, 1949, 41,000 copies were distributed. The later innovation of the "Midland 'Red' Observers Club" quickly

grew to 3,000. The 3,000th member being Master K. Barnes of Duke Street, Birmingham. About the same time, Driver A. Littleford and Conductor H. Cook, a Sutton crew, were complimented for being most obliging "in helping a woman passenger who had boarded the wrong bus, and the Conductor displayed remarkably good humour in the midst of a crowded vehicle. Everyone round about remarked on their kindness and cheerfulness as a rare occurrence nowadays".

A new AEC Regal with Burlingham body owned by Don Everall of Wolverhampton is shown at Bromford Racecourse in 1947. (K. A. F. Brewin)

Chapter Five

Sutton garage grows, Lichfield garage opens

All-time mileage records

Further quotes from the MR Staff Bulletins, with permission of the Kithead Trust, Droitwich, and loaned by David Jenkins, stated in the January, 1950 issue, "All-time records for mileage operated and passengers carried were established by the company in 1949". There was a six million miles increase over 1948, with 13 million more passengers, bringing a 1949 total of 438,474,279 passengers carried. The fleet of 1,732 of coaches and buses was increased by 194, though a number of other vehicles were "taken off the road at the end of their operating life". Another sign of growth was the "introduction of 24 new services, a reinstatement of 14 others suspended during the war, and increase of frequency of 304 services". Some year! The fuel tax in 1949 was 9d on a gallon of petrol or fuel oil. The BMMO contributed £250,000 to the Exchequer that way. Miss C.M. Tucker, mentioned earlier, left the company in the winter of 1949 after 28 years' service. She was married on Boxing Day, 26th December. Miss Tucker was mentioned by a number of people. The General Manager, Mr. D.M. Sinclair, was awarded the C.B.E. in the 1950 New Year Honours list. Although the 1949 Midland Red Accident Record revealed Sutton retaining the bottom place for the third year running, local driver A. Ashworth received a passenger's compliment about his driving "on dreadful icey roads, and in particular the driver of the bus from Boldmere this morning. From the front seat I had a very good view of the condition of the road and was amazed at the manner in which he managed to avoid skids, although the road showed many obvious marks of previous skids".

Sutton garage extension

The major event at Sutton's Midland Red garage in 1950 was the extension. The triple authorship, two volumes on the Midland Red, notes on page 171 : "Material delays of post-war Britain considerably delayed overdue extensions to Sutton garage which, by early 1949 had an allocation of 73. However, on 31st January, 1950, an extension was opened and this increased the capacity to one hundred vehicles. The garage was now extremely long with a rear entrance and remained virtually unaltered when it passed to the WMPTE on 3rd December, 1973. The initial actual number of vehicles at Sutton was probably about 49 and this had risen to 70 by 1948, just reaching three figures by 1956, and then gradually decreasing to around 60 from 1967". The Diamond Jubilee brochure advises readers on page 12 "it was not until 1950 that the company was able to see the completion of the first of the building schemes which had been put in hand since

Some Sutton Coldfield MR bus crews taking a tea break in the upper Holland Road canteen. (Tom Carey Collection)

The Sutton BMMO Engineering Superintendent Mr N.L.Cole (Left), discussing technical details with Engineering Foreman Mr F.Y.Wood (Right) and garage Hand, Mr A.Salmanis. (Tom Carey Collection)

the war ended. This was an extension to the existing garage at Sutton Coldfield". The Traffic Superintendent at Sutton, Mr. F.A. Kerrison reported in the March, 1950 Staff Bulletin that "The football team continues to maintain its winning ways, and once again reached the final of the Director's Cup". Sutton beat Hereford 5-1. Sutton's chief scorer was 'hat trick' Whittles.

John Wem started at Sutton garage on the engineering side, when the extension had been open six months, but the "rear doors of the garage were not completed and there was no access to the rear of the garage. During 1950 the road from South Parade to the garage was built which meant a lot of pile driving to make the bridge over Plants Brook. Piles were driven in the ground one night and by next morning they had sunk and had to be done again. The old garage itself was built on a bog so it was virtually floated on rafts and piles. Over the years a crack appeared across the garage floor between the old and new garage. So when the buses ran over it you could see it move up and down. Before the entrance was made, buses had to reverse off Upper Holland Road which caused quite a congestion when the buses were filled up with fuel, then having to turn round. In snow or when the stream was in flood, the 1950 sunken workshop with 6 pits had to be baled out each morning as water used to seep in through the wall". Mr Wem's very first job as a garage hand was to help "start a petrol engine. There were no starter motors in those days. My job was to put my hand over the carburettor to choke it while two men pulled on a rope on the starting handle". Tom Carey joined the Midland Red as a Conductor in 1950 at the Upper Holland Road garage. His early memories include "a fleet of mainly double- deck diesel vehicles, being the company's own make front loaders. There were 2 single deckers and one

double deck petrol. At that time the wooden seats installed during WWII had been replaced by upholstered seats". By June, 1950, negotiations were well in hand for the provision of a reinforced concrete building to accommodate the new sports club. In that same month the Red Engineering Notes anticipated "Midland Red employees as a whole will be interested to learn that on Thursday, 1st June, 1950, the first day upon which the new regulations took effect, the first Midland Red single deck omnibus to be built to the newly permitted increased length of 30' was placed in service. The vehicle, which is 8' in width, is of the now-familiar 'S' type with underfloor engine, built throughout to the Company's own exclusive designs, and seats 44 passengers, 4 more than the normal Midland Red single decker ... It is believed that we were the first operating company in the country actually to place on service a vehicle built to the new dimensions on the very first day permitted in the new regulations, a fact of which we can perhaps take not a little pride!" The double

The Midland "Red" Travel Bureau on the Parade was close to South Parade. (Tom Carey Collection)

deck omnibuses could be increased in length on the same day from 26' to 27'. According to Mr. Keeley "all single-deckers built since the war were extended to the new length, allowing 44 seats. Nearly 500 buses were involved".

1951 opening of Sutton Club Room

Sutton Garage's own Club Room was opened on Monday, 9th July, 1951 by the General Manager, when he unlocked the premises. The facilities included "two billiard tables, and refreshment area". Speaking of the local Sports-Social Committee, David Jenkins wrote of them as a "Hard working lot in doing the duties in their own time. Two dances each year in Sutton Coldfield Town Hall, with 350/400 attending, and many Council Officials and Councillors present with the

General Manager and other Red management. Any profit was sent to the Spastic Society. Vera Lynn attended once to accept the cheque on behalf of the charity".....Mrs Maggie Bennett, writing about her father, Bob 'Cracker' Burns, said "he was a founder member of the MR Club off South Parade, and began as a Red employee in 1934, when the garage opened". Mr. Burns organised staff excursions to race meetings including Royal Ascot. He tried to get the race course re-opened in Sutton Park. In the list of Upper Holland Road drivers her step-mother remembered, was Larry Boughton., who was half owner of the Parade Cafe., previously owned by A.T. Hastilows. Mrs. Bennett worked in the cafe. Apparently Maggie sat on ATH's knee and Bobby drove for MR and Tudor Coaches. Other Sutton MR Club activities as touched on before were the Christmas Party for employees' children, plus outings to the pantomime and circus.

Something of the generation gap was shown between Sutton's teenagers and their elders on 6th February, 1952. With some friends we had arranged to meet that night at the Empress cinema on the Parade. When we met, to our surprise and anger the pictures had been cancelled because of the death of King George VIth. It seems we had no respect for the King and the Royal Family or the feelings of the adults, who generally mourned his death. The Coronation of Queen Elizabeth II was held 16 months later. A number of people have referred to the 1952 three page spread pp 7-9 on the Sutton garage in the Staff Bulletin. Editor W.H. Pirie, spoke of Driver G.A. Horton, with 32 years service on the Red, and the second longest service belonged to Conductor S.J. Smith with three months less. Five other employees at Sutton with 25 years service or more were "Mr. F.G. Smith, Garage Traffic Assistant; Mr. H. Norris,

Mr.F.Smith takes over the 'takings' in the Cash Office.
(Tom Carey Collection)

Driver; Mr. W. T. Garner, Driver; Mr. A. E. Lakin, Driver; and Mr. F. Robinson, Garage Traffic Assistant". Mr. Robinson was known as 'Daylight' because it was alleged that he could not drive in the dark. "He resigned early" according to Mr. Jenkins "to move to Jersey with his daughter and son-in-law". Reviewing bus services provided, Mr. Pine noted "The services are mainly very heavy ones, connecting Birmingham with Sutton via the main road, with Sutton via New Oscott, with Streetly, Mere Green, Canwell, Lichfield and Burton. There are also a number of local services in the Erdington and Sutton localities, operated from the garage".

The MRs most persistent bus spotter

A 16-year old Sutton Coldfield schoolboy at the time, probably knew the local bus timetables as well as some of the Red employees. After successfully completing a three-year "bus spotting" task of all the company's 1,804 buses, Malcolm Cooper, a Bishop Vesey's Grammar School pupil, received a presentation at a special ceremony attended by the General Manager. Malcolm, who is now an enthusiastic member of the Witton preservation group, was complimented for his "extraordinary feat of tenacity and skill". Malc, was one of 10,000 recipients to receive the Midland Red Spotters badge, but the only one to have seen each vehicle. One of our contributors, David Jenkins, a Sutton Traffic Inspector in June, 1952, was praised for assisting a young passenger who missed her bus at Erdington. In 1952, I was 17 years old, and frequently used our local Midland Red services, walking past the garage on my way to church in Duke Street. The Midland Red was an integral part of Sutton Coldfield life, providing a more regular service to Birmingham and Lichfield than the train, though at times, slower. Even so, any increase in fares, were

Two of Sutton Garage's longest serving staff, (Left) Driver G.A.Horton and Conductor Mr.S.J.Smith, both with 32 years service at the time. (Tom Carey Collection)

subject to much derisive comment in the Royal Town. David told me "Sutton Coldfield Council were very helpful. All the local routes, bus stops, terminal points and turning arrangements were always discussed and agreed before an application was made. This assisted the passage of the application. These discussions also always involved the police". Coming back to a rise in fares, David was at the sharp end of public opinion. He continued, "However, any fare increase application was objected to by the Council". David said, "Mr. Arthur Spencer was the Surveyor's Assistant whom we liaised with in connection with fares, routes and stops. He was very helpful taking a more than normal interest in transport and transport matters".

Glasgow and Ludlow recruits

From this point I am going to focus more on the characters that worked at the Sutton Red Garage, though significant changes will be mentioned. Tom Carey takes on the story of staff who came via the Vesey Road Hostel Scheme. "The recruitment van was sent to Glasgow. About 15 recruits arrived. These lads used their visit to Birmingham as a holiday, they just didn't want to work. One in particular I remember well. I was detailed to train him as a conductor. On meeting him on the first morning, I asked his name and he replied, "call me 'Buck'". He would not collect the fares, smoked continually upstairs and down. He asked me what the huts were in Rectory Road. I told him Good Hope Hospital. He realised it was next to the cemetery. Next journey he called out, "Good Hope and next door, no hope!" After passing out, or completing his initial training, on his first morning an Inspector found him asleep on the bus. No fares collected. Last of Buck". Mr Carey has vivid memories of Ludlow staff transported to ease the

These "Sunken Workshops" in Sutton Garage formed part of the Dock. This area was known to flood after prolonged rain. (Tom Carey Collection)

employment shortage at Upper Holland Road. "A bus used to arrive from Ludlow, carrying drivers and conductors on their day off, also on occasions Traffic Superintendents and Inspectors portions of duties which we were unable to cover, were allocated to them. Sometimes they would operate a full day duty, but most times they would work 3 or 4 hours and sit in the canteen and maybe do a little portion in the afternoon. They would return to Ludlow about 1900 hours". Tom tells a story against himself when conducting on the 107 route, proceeding down Newtown Row. "Suddenly I sneezed and my false teeth which I had just acquired went flying onto the gutter. The driver had slowed due to traffic and I jumped off, ran back about 100 yards, picked them up, wrapped them in my handkerchief and put them in my pocket. Flagged the next bus down and told the driver to follow that 107 bus" Mr. F.A. Kerrison in his regular "post from the outposts" on Sutton mentioned in the November 1952 item, the death of driver S. Luckham, whose wife was a conductress at Sutton garage in WWII. In the same issue driver K.A. Burton and conductor A.S. Dennis were commended for showing kindness to a lame 77 year old lady and her daughter from Chester Road to Lichfield. On the 12th November, at the Castle Hotel, Tamworth, drivers from the Tamworth and Sutton Coldfield Garages were presented with awards they had gained in the competitions organised by the Royal Society for the Prevention of Accidents in 1950 and 1951. The Tamworth staff who had Bars to 15 year broaches were Messrs A.W. Farrant; H.R. Wileman; E. Eden; S. James A.G. Dorman; S.W. Davis. Their colleagues at Sutton were: A.A. Somerville and P.E. Barnes. In 1953, the strong Midland Red presence within the 91 member Midland Branch of The Omnibus Society was strengthened with the presidency being taken over by Mr. D.M. Sinclair, C.B.E. In addition to the BMMO and Cos General Manager, the Red was represented by Messrs. A.G.C. Baker; P.L. Hardy; J.C. Fenton; J.W. Oakley; R.A. Mills; D.W. Woodhouse and G.H. Stone in executive or committee positions. Although Sutton was nearly always at or near to the bottom of the Red garage accident league, Driver G.L. Siviter demonstrated how observant he and his colleagues could be. He noticed a private car careering towards him, without a driver. Making his bus safe he "jumped from his cab, ran towards the oncoming car, jumped into the driving seat, steered the car into the side of the road and stopped it, before any damage was done; all this probably took less than it takes to describe it on paper. For his quick reaction to what might have developed into a dangerous situation, Mr. Siviter deserves high praise".

Cornish memories of Sutton garage

A former Sutton Driver wrote to the Staff Bulletin from his native Cornwall, saying "Since I have been down here working for another company, I have realised what a splendid go-ahead firm the Midland Red is. There are no social activities here, neither is there the friendliness of between-garage functions for which the Midland Red is so noted. In fact it is very 'hum-drum'. I have personally passed B.M.M.O. coaches on tour in parts of Devon and Cornwall, and found myself looking longingly after them and wishing I was back with the staff at Sutton Coldfield, and the dirt of good old Birmingham!" Over in Staffordshire, Driver S. James

The Sutton Garage Waybill Analysis Team are left to right: Mrs E.M.Griffiths, Mrs K.Dodd, Miss B.Gould, Mrs J Reynolds (standing), Mrs I.Wilson, Mrs D.P.Walker and Miss L.Smith. (Tom Carey Collection)

of the Tamworth Garage arranged a March 1953 visit of the Midland Red Symphony Orchestra at Wilnecote Parish Hall, where they gave an excellent concert to raise funds for the Old Folks Party. Tamworth Garage gained runners-up position in Division 'A' of the 1952-53 season Midland Red Football League, Sutton finished fifth of the nine teams having played 15; won 7; lost 6 and drawn 2.

Coronation of Queen Elizabeth II

The Coronation of Queen Elizabeth II was an important day in Lichfield and Sutton, on 2nd June, 1953. The Staff Bulletin in May, conveyed the Friendly Midland Red's "Loyal Greetings to Her Majesty from the Midland Red Family". People's intense interest in the Coronation led to Mrs. Helen Ramm organising two railway outings from Trent Valley area stations to see the Coronation decorations in London. Quoting from Cross City Connections, p. 19, "The outings included a 3-hour coach tour in the capital to see the preparation for the big day. After the tour, supper was available at an Oxford Street Restaurant for a further 5/3 on top of the train/coach fare of 22/-. Mrs. Ramm's railway outings became very popular, continuing until shortly before she died in 1986". Broad's Travel Bureau booked two Tudor Rose coaches to take Sutton and Birmingham people for a view of the London decorations and Coronation route. Practically all Midland Red Garages and Booking and Enquiry Offices throughout the area were specially decorated for the Coronation period. The design and general arrangements were in the hands of Mr. L.F.P. Trueman, Publicity Superintendent, in co-operation with the local staffs. Upper Holland Road Garage was one of eighteen selected in a Bulletin photo-call of some Red outposts

"Dressed" for the Coronation. The Sutton Traffic Supt. F.A. Kerrison and his staff were congratulated on transporting children to Sutton Park for a Coronation event. "In view of the inclement weather that day and at our request, you kindly provided us with eleven additional buses, which must have meant a considerable amount of organisation on your part, for which we are most grateful". Such State occasions as a Coronation or royal wedding gain media attention but well done routine, every-day work was what Mr. Sinclair wrote about in the Bulletin and in his memo-type letter to staff.

Compliments to Lichfield and Tamworth staff

It was with the build-up towards the Coronation that Miss Olive Wassall at the Company's Bore Street office in Lichfield, seemed to exemplify the GMs picture of an employee who encouraged the public to return to use the Midland Red services again and again. A customer wrote "...at all times I have found her most efficient, conscientious and very courteous... In conclusion I would like to say that she is a credit to your Company". However, amongst the happiness around at the time of the Coronation, the death of Sutton Driver, Mr. W.T. Reid, well known as the local secretary of the Sick and Dividend Society and member of the Benevolent Fund Committee, brought sorrow to many Sutton staff, that 1953 June. An interesting item in the Birmingham Gazette reported that one of the Tamworth Garage Inspectors, Mr. T. Brammer, was adjudged to be the Tamworth Council Tenants' Champion Gardener. Incidentally, the 1953 cricket season for Tamworth Garage was described as "a very good season, played 17, won 12, lost 5". Driver J. Warwick was noted for taking 57 wickets

The Sutton Coldfield BMMO 1934 opened Garage in Upper Holland Road on a rainy day. In their two volume account of the company, Messrs Gray, Keeley and Seale wrote. " The four bay frontage included some ornamental brickwork, less 'decorative' but neat in appearance." (Tom Carey Collection)

and scoring 136 runs during the season. Driver Lunn scored 143. Towards the end of September, 1953, Technical and West Midland journalists viewed the Midland Red's latest range of vehicles designed and built entirely by the Company at its works in Carlyle Road, Birmingham. The most popular of the 3 was the latest 44-seater single decker designated the 'S.14. The 'C.4' was the latest long-distance coach, with 32 seats. The third new addition was a 58-seater double-decker known as the 'D.7'. A number of this latter type were already in service at the time of the press visit. Commenting on the 'S.14' a BMMO spokesman wrote "These new features, it is believed, represent a world advance in design, for most of them are incorporated in a public service vehicle for the first time". The "Modern Transport" journalist said "BMMO designs continue to be in the van of engineering progress; the under- floor engine developments among British manufacturers gained immense impetus from the successful examples running in the Midland Red fleet. Other pioneering work has been done on independent front springing, rubber suspension, disc brakes and above all, Monocoque construction. A new prototype, the 'S.14' is a notable vehicle... the new 'C.3' and 'C.4' coaches and 'D.7' double-decker are also vehicles of distinction and comfort". Mr. Keeley had his own views on the S.14 and D.7 vehicles. Although he acknowledged the production S.14 buses were technically advanced, they were simplified in specification and the passengers may have been less impressed. Interior finish was not so good in an endeavour to save weight. For the same reason they had single rear wheels and "rode like a cart" . The D.7 buses were also "weight conscious". A friend of Mr. Keeley described them as "pop rivets and hardboard".

Later the D. 7s had their seating increased with 5 more upstairs. Malcolm confided that meant "people like me could not fit in the seats". He continued "All this weight and capacity activity related to the worsening financial position".

Decrease in passengers, increase in mileage

With 122 new buses added to the fleet in 1953, the vehicles totalled 1,818, the total annual mileage increased by 1,074,619 to 76,131,792, but the company carried 9¼ millions less passengers. Despite continuing staff shortages, 14 new services were introduced, and 156 existing services increased. Mark Priest's fleet list of Sutton vehicles 1953-1959 is included at this point in Wheels around Sutton. The March 1954 Staff Bulletin had a centre-spread on Midland House, the company's new Registered Offices at 1, Vernon Road, Edgbaston, erected in the 1860s as a private hospital. The Carlyle Works property was situated immediately at the rear of Midland House, where the General Manager and many H.Q. personnel were based. The Midland House move enabled the Midland Red to relinquish some accommodation in the Bearwood vicinity detached from the main Bearwood property which had been used as offices. On May 28th a Midland Red personality, well known in the Sutton Coldfield and Birmingham areas, was presented with a clock in the Sutton staff canteen by Driver J.C. Hooper. Traffic Superintendent Mr. F.A. Kerrison, at Sutton joined the Company in June, 1928. Formerly on the clerical staff at Sutton Coldfield he was appointed Resident Inspector at Upper Holland Road early in 1936. There is some disagreement between the Staff Bulletin and David Jenkins dates, noted earlier. The Bulletin reported "Mr. Kerrison had therefore been responsible for Traffic Department affairs in the Sutton Coldfield locality for more than eighteen of his 26 years with the Company". Mr. Kerrison's representation of the Transport and General Workers' Union at Sutton garage was appreciated.

Lichfield's own BMMO garage

A later report from Sutton Garage Correspondent, Mr. E.L. Blunden, wrote that "Sutton employees would like to take this opportunity of welcoming their new Traffic Superintendent, Mr. J.W. Comelio to Sutton Garage. Mr. Comelio was at one time Secretary and Chairman of the Sutton Sports and Social Club, and all wish him well on his return to his old Garage". Not long after Mr. Comeliols promotion, Mr. H. Smith, from Sutton, was appointed Traffic Superintendent, and Mr. A.D. Wormington the Engineering Superintendent, at the Lichfield Garage, opened on 17th September, 1954. The two volume Midland Red History described the "garage as small, modern and attractive, incorporating two storey office accommodation on the frontage ... The garage capacity was 30 but only sixteen were allocated at the opening... The initial allocation included one 'SLR' coach, in later years replaced by an 'ONC'. Half the post war stock was in the early years, 1948/49 "S 8's although, of course, examples of all types were to be found in small numbers". Mr. H. Smith's connection with the Upper Holland Road garage is spoken of in the 3-page spread on the new garage in the November 1954 Staff Bulletin. At the time of the article he had "nearly 23 years service... commencing as a Conductor in the Black Country in January 1932 and was afterwards transferred to

Sutton Coldfield Garage. He was appointed Traffic Inspector there in 1941, and served in that district and in that capacity ... until his Lichfield appointment. Mr. A.D. Wormington joined the Red in 1943 at Bromsgrove with subsequent appointments at Leamington Spa and Redditch going for Engineering Superintendent training in December 1953".

In addition to the 112 service, Lichfield operated the No. 765 to Coventry and the No. 825 to Stafford, with those 3 services in 1954 keeping "nine" buses fully occupied each day. There were a number of significant "local routes connecting Lichfield with various villages round about, and then there were important Works Services to Rugeley, Stafford etc". The new garage came within the Coalville division from the Traffic side and the Engineering department was part of the Birmingham area. The garage was a mile from the city centre on the Trent Valley Estate, and its postal address was Trent Valley Road. There was an Enquiry Office incorporated in the premises. Reference has been made to the Enquiry Office in Lichfield, at 19 Bore Street occupied since 1949. The BMMO had an office "on the opposite side of the road since 1946".

New features in Lichfield garage

The Lichfield Mercury supplied further background data. Local builders J.R. Deacon Ltd "began the garage 18 months ago, but a shortage of bricks delayed its completion. The garage housed its first bus two weeks" before the official opening, "when Mr. Sinclair C.B.E. introduced the Mayor of Lichfield [Alderman A.L. Garratt J.P.], who severed the tape to formally open the premises ... When in full working order it is anticipated employment will be for between 80-100

The opening Ceremony at the BMMO Garage on Trent Valley Road, Lichfield on 17th September 1954. The Mayor of Lichfield, (Alderman. A. L. Garratt J.P) severed the tape, after being introduced by Mr. D.Sinclair C.B.E. (2nd from right) Mr. A.D.Worthington in the white coat was the Engineering Superintendent at Lichfield, with his Traffic Superintendant colleague Mr 'Time Table' H. Smith, fifth from the right. (Mrs. E. Smith)

Lichfield citizens, including 27 drivers and 27 conductors ... Although one of the Company's smaller garages, its new features contain an automatic washer ... Local routes were formally covered principally from Sutton and Tamworth". A Red advertisement at the time drew Mercury readers' attention to the daily coach services that called at Lichfield for Manchester and North of England and Cheltenham for London and South Coast resorts. Mrs. E. Smith, widow of Mr. H. Smith, confirmed that he "was Traffic Superintendent at the Lichfield Garage from the time it opened in 1954 until it closed in 1971. After the Garage closed, he was in charge, and ran the booking office in the Bus Station, until his retirement in 1975. He was known as 'Time Table' Smith". Ken Bullock who had nearly 40 years service with the BMMO at Digbeth, Sutton and Lichfield, advised me that Mr. Smith was so familiar with the company's timetable and services "he had the timetable committed to memory". Ken defined the Lichfield depot "as a friendly garage. It was a piece of cake after the intensity of services from Digbeth and Sutton. On the Sutton to Birmingham route for instance, the driver had 37 minutes to cover the 49 stops". Mr. Bullock found the Lichfield garage life so much more relaxed from working in the larger depots. Ken's wife, Margaret, told me she was a conductress at Sutton in the late 1940s, before they married. "Work was fun. In those days, we helped each other, as a team. You were kept on your feet all day. In a day I could issue up to 1,000 tickets and take less than £10.00 back to the office! I recall going to work every day with clean hands. Even with the 15 minutes booking in time, I sometimes had insufficient time to wash my hands after duty, going with dirty green hands from handling bronze coins. My first wage packet was £3 1s 3d. with overtime in 1948". One of the Lichfield garage correspondents was Mr. Frank Withers who was a member of the bus crew on the first one out in 1954 and last vehicle out on the closing day in 1971.

A Bedford OB, with Duple body, owned by Mason's Coachways of Walsall. (K. A. F. Brewin)

Chapter Six

Financial fragility and engineering prominence reduced

Lichfield's friendly depot spirit

The publication in the Lichfield Mercury at the end of March, 1995, of Mrs. E. Smith's print of the Lichfield garage opening in September, 1954, brought in much interest with a number of the 36 men identified. Mrs. Smith advised me "my husband is 5th from right, back row in uniform". Mr. A.D. Wormington, the Engineering Superintendent in the white coat stood next to the Mayor. The BMMO General Manager is the last but one on the right. According to local newspaper readers, many of the gentlemen in the picture were in local businesses and active politicians, whose names are still well known in Lichfield. Some readers of "Wheels around Sutton" may well recognise their names. The family atmosphere within Lichfield garage is commented upon by Frank Campagna, writing from Italy. Mr. Campagna served as a conductor and driver at Lichfield, later moving to Tamworth. He wrote "At Lichfield we were like a big family with a lot of friends like John Stock. Frank Withers, Freddy Wood and that wonderful man Mr. Harry Smith as a superintendent. We used to call him, Mr. Timetable. He was a gentleman". Going on to speak of the work carried out from the Trent Valley Road garage, Frank continued, "We used to do the S71 Tower Estate Mere Green to Six Ways, Erdington, all day long". Lichfield was also involved with the S76, S67, 102, 103 and 112. He recalled the "Lichfield and Stafford Town services, like the Highfield and Richerscote, also the Coventry hourly service, at 11.20, 12.20, 13.20, then at 16.20, 17.20 and 18.20". "There were some joint services which operated quite successfully", commented David Jenkins, "though there were occasional outbursts and hostilities, mainly due to clash of personalities. However, notwithstanding those minor irritations, vehicles, ticket issuing machines were freely interchanged. Lichfield garage did take over the operation of some Sutton services as a 'temporary' measure, but were not returned until closure of Lichfield. The transfer of services to Lichfield was due to staffing problems at Sutton Coldfield". David thought local relationships between BMMO & Co with Upper Holland Road residents were "not too bad up to mid/late 1950s, with the build-up of the fleet, more early and late services - and less considerable staff". He also thought "more staff with cars and change of ownership of the nearby houses", were other contributing factors. The "situation improved when fuel pumps moved from the front to the rear of the garage". Ray Jennings, a Sutton driver, said "it was a good garage, but you couldn't breathe for exhaust fumes. There was so much smoke about around 5.0 a.m. it enveloped the garage. There was a good club and good canteen". At the Midland Red Golden Jubilee Dinner on November 25th, 1954 in the Grand Hotel, Birmingham, local garage areas were represented by the Mayor of Lichfield, the Deputy Mayor of

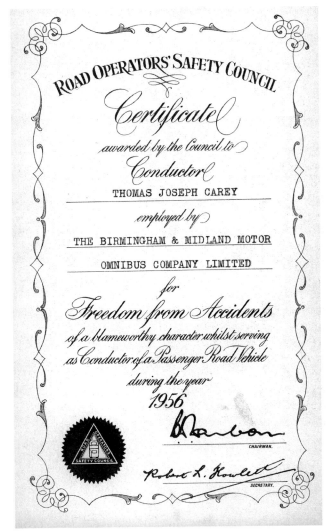

One of Mr. Carey's valued possessions.

Sutton Coldfield, and the Sheriff of Lichfield. During a response by the Lord Mayor of Birmingham, Alderman J.R. Balmer he said "Last week I visited Sutton Coldfield to see the first 'bus converted into a vehicle to carry old folk, leave on its maiden voyage. I was informed that this 'bus was being driven by a Midland Red driver who had volunteered to drive without any thought of reward. That shows the spirit of the staff of the Midland Red and is indeed a very fine gesture". Roger De Boer mentions the welfare bus a little later but Malcolm Keeley reminded me, "This was not a Midland Red bus but was kept at the depot. It was actually rather interesting, being an ex- London Transport AEC"Q" with a side engine". At the opening of the new Carlyle Works, that November, 1954 afternoon, the Lord Mayor of Birmingham stepped in at short notice, when the Minister of Transport, Mr. Boyd Carpenter, could not make it, to open the new BMMO premises. At the Midland Red Golden Jubilee Dinner on November 25th, 1954 in the Grand Hotel,

The Lord Mayor of Birmingham, Alderman J.R.Balmer, visited Sutton Coldfield Midland Red garage to see the first bus (CGJ188) converted into a vehicle to carry old folk, leave on its maiden voyage in November, 1954. It was the last London Q Type Coach. (M. Gottschalk)

Birmingham, local garage areas were represented by the Mayor of Lichfield, the Deputy Mayor of Sutton Coldfield, and the Sheriff of Lichfield. During a response by the Lord Mayor of Birmingham, Alderman J.R. Balmer he said "Last week I visited Sutton Coldfield to see the first 'bus converted into a vehicle to carry old folk, leave on its maiden voyage. I was informed that this 'bus was being driven by a Midland Red driver who had volunteered to drive without any thought of reward. That shows the spirit of the staff of the Midland Red and is indeed a very fine gesture". Roger De Boer mentions the   .'fare bus a little later but Malcolm Keeley reminded me, "T ıis was not a Midland Red bus but was kept at the depot. It was actually rather interesting, being an ex- London Transport AECP with a side engine". At the opening of the new Carlyle Works, that November, 1954 afternoon, the Lord Mayor of Birmingham stepped in at short notice, when the Minister of Transport, Mr. Boyd Carpenter, could not make it, to open the new B.M.M.O. premises.

Midland Red support at 1955 rail crash

The 101st issue of the Staff Bulletin in February 1955, recorded the appreciation of the railway and police for the Sutton Coldfield Red staff at the scene of the train crash at Sutton Coldfield station on the afternoon of Sunday, 23rd January that year. The Chief Commercial Manager at Euston Station, London, wrote "I wish to thank you for the splendid assistance you and your company gave us in the provision of manpower and equipment to help in rescue work on the occasion of the regrettable train accident at Sutton

Coldfield". The Chief Constable of Warwickshire spoke of "The rapidity with which your staff provided transport and their ready offer of rescue equipment was greatly appreciated by the local police, and made their task a great deal easier. I would be grateful if you convey the appreciation of this constabulary to the gentlemen concerned". On Monday and Tuesday, 24th and 25th the Four Oaks rail route was closed to traffic. The Birmingham Evening Mail of Monday, 24th January, reported "that two extra buses were provided by the Digbeth garage, and 5 by the Lichfield garage of the Midland Red company ... Buses from Lichfield City station went to Shenstone, Blake Street or Sutton Park, to link up with the emergency service from there to Birmingham". Few transport enthusiasts appear to be aware that on those two days, the London Midland Region of British Railways reopened the former Sutton Town station in Midland Drive, which had closed on the 1st January, 1925, 30 years before. Further details of the 1879 opened station, a public petition in 1924 to try and keep it open and the surprise of Saltley engine driver Bill Alcock is quoted in Cross City Connections on page 27, when the morning Sutton Park local commuter train to Birmingham New Street, pulled up in Sutton Town station, that January day. David Jenkins told me "We, [at the Midland Red], in common with many other operators, had an obligation to provide alternative bus services. Railway cover had first call on our resources! Service was provided to Birmingham - mainly - but not well used. No recollection of service to Midland Drive ... My experience of any replacement bus services, whether due to accident cover or track

Passengers alight from D7, VHA 426, on a S71 service in Reddicap Heath Road, in January, 1960. (M. Gottschalk)

repairs/relaying, were not very successful - rail passengers appeared to make their own arrangements". A popular figure of the Sutton garage who left in 1955 was the canteen supervisor Mrs. Florence Williams, who lived in Tamworth. The staff report added that Mrs. Williams "enjoyed her job and was very popular with staff. She had accompanied her husband abroad on his duties of army service. Her knowledge of Hindustani was appreciated by some of the Indian Garage Hand Mechanics". Mr. Jenkins told me about a couple of staff. "Driver T. Orton had been a Japanese prisoner of war. He had reduced from 14 stone to half that weight. For many years he had to attend a tropical disease centre for treatment which could last a week or more. He never grumbled, he was very reliable". I was amused by his way of getting into the spirit of driving the coach when in a certain area of the U.K. David continued: "On Scottish Tours he would discard his made-to-measure Tour suit and don a kilt!" Presumably there was a Midland Red tartan! David recalled that Sutton garage "had many members of one family. A mother with two daughters; 3 sisters and a son of one of them; 3 brothers; and a number of husbands and wives", were some examples that came to him.

Less passengers, introduction of OM vehicles

In the second of the two volume history of the Midland Red, referring to the early and mid 19050s, we are informed "Passenger figures began to drop as more people were able to afford private motoring, while the impact of television slashed evening traffic". An important factor for pushing passengers towards private motoring was the regular fare increases from February 1951. Midland Red management seeking to resolve the continuing rising staff costs and

inability to recruit sufficient bus crews, introduced a controversial policy in 1956. The Diamond Jubilee publication, p. 16 advises "... on July 1st, saw the first service operated by the company with 'one-man vehicles' in the Hereford area. This type of operation was to grow over the years, and by the middle of 1964 over eighty 'one-man vehicles were in service at seventeen different garages'". The Jubilee booklet includes information on two local garages in 1956, p. 16 "In the department of 'bricks and mortar', extensions of the Bromsgrove and Tamworth garages were completed, and new first-floor offices at Sutton Coldfield". The General Manager in March, 1956, was taking his staff to task about bad workmanship with a finger especially pointed towards drivers "failing to stop to pick up intending passengers". But, in the same Staff Bulletin a lady passenger from Brixham, Devon, complimented Sutton driver Mr. E.G. Taylor. "Yesterday morning I travelled from Sutton Coldfield to Birmingham on the 11.30 a.m. Canwell bus, 3478. Unfortunately, owing to the dense fog, he struck the rear of a stationery van causing slight damage to the front wing of the bus. I want to inform you that he avoided a really bad accident through his promptness in pulling up. There was no question of carelessness, as visibility was practically nil".

World's largest box of chocolates

In 1956, an Inspector of Police in Qatar, in Eastern Arabia, Mr. J.B. Hay, advised the Staff Bulletin that he was a former Upper Holland Road employee with the Midland Red, noting two 'SLR' coaches in Qatar, were about "to inaugurate a 'bus service, and the two ex-Midland Red coaches will be the first to operate ... May I be permitted to convey my best wishes to yourself and the company, particularly those at Sutton depot". Mr. Jenkins remembered a now deceased Sutton garage couple "who had an engagement of some 10 years - they did marry and continued at Sutton until retirement, they were Norman Hodges and Elsie Johnson". The October Staff Bulletin told how Driver Hodges "saw a 25lb box of chocolates in Coombes sweet shop window on the corner of South Parade and the Parade. He went in to buy the chocolates for Conductress Johnson only to be told it was a dummy". The bulletin of October 1956 goes on "His disappointment was brief, however, for the firm using the box as an advertisement agreed to make one specially for him". The event "created history in the confectionery trade by obtaining what was described as 'the largest box of chocolates in the world'". Mr. Fred Leonard Bacchus was featured in the November 1956 Staff Bulletin. He joined the company in "August 1918 ... When the second World War ended Mr. Bacchus became a full-time Bus-and-Coach Driver ... In August 1945 he became Resident Engineer or Garage Engineering Superintendent at the Cradley Heath Garage, transferring to Sutton Coldfield in May, 1946. This position he held until 1949 when, following a serious illness, he was instructed by his doctor to seek an outdoor occupation ... returning to his former position as Engineering Inspector on 1st July of that year". The Sutton Coldfield News published a poem by David Jenkins on the recently introduced street lighting. "The Sutton Road new lighting to us proves most exciting, As underneath its yellow glare we could only stand and stare, While waiting for a Midland Red, We found all buses were instead, As they travelled Sutton way, A curious ghostly shade of grey". David later said "the colour was rather more chocolate than grey". The Diamond Jubilee booklet referred to the "Suez crisis at the end of 1956 bringing fuel rationing which led to a 5% reduction in stage carriage services and 50% to express services, private hire,

tours and excursions". The GM commented in a later Staff Bulletin that more people had travelled on the company's buses during the 'crisis'. In February, 1957, a sports celebrity assisted in providing an "excellent evening's entertainment at the Sutton Social Club ... This was an exhibition of snooker given by Rex Williams, Britain's youngest snooker player ... A collection at the "do", with receipts from a raffle, totalling £50.00 was sent to the National Spastics Society". Continuing on the sporting scene, the Midland Red Ladies' Darts Team were at the top of Sutton and District Darts league.

MR Scout Jamboree contributions

A large event held in Sutton Coldfield in August 1957, was the Scout Jamboree in Sutton Park, a celebration of the Jubilee of the movement. Midland Red vehicles were used extensively in conveying the Scouts themselves, and thousands of visitors, to and from Birmingham and Sutton Coldfield, and also to destinations much further afield. As an appreciation, the Boy Scouts Association presented an engraved testimonial that was received at the Red' central offices. It read "the Boy Scouts Association wish to express their gratitude to the Midland Red Omnibus Co. Ltd., for their help and support in the celebration of the centenary of the Birth of their Founder and the Jubilee of the Scout Movement". During the period of the Jamboree the Red "supplied about 85 vehicles for private-hire assignments, principally to convey scouts from other lands to the Shakespeare country, and to London". A comparison of the local railways involvement in the same week long event is on pp 49-54 in Cross City Connections, under "Railway dimensions of the Jamboree" with 7 pictures and data from the Scout HQ archives. Bescot engine driver, Terry Wright, informed me in 1996 that a luggage off-loading platform was

An Ex-Birmingham City Transport pre-war Daimler, type COG registration CVP 222, is parked near Sutton Methodist Church, the rear entrance to the BMMO garage, with "The Empress" in the distance. March 1962. (M. Gottschalk)

Walsall Corporation Leyland Atlantean, 841 FDH, at the Victoria Road, Sutton terminus for the No.6 route to Walsall, seen in 1960. (M. Gottschalk)

built on the down side line near to Streetly station for the scouts. He recalled travelling past it as a fireman. He saw scout camping equipment on the platform with scouting personnel on the temporary 1957 structure.

Miss Wassell and Mrs. Wright are shown in the Bore Street, Lichfield Enquiry Office 'selling travel', one of 17 pictures in the 3-page Staff Bulletin feature on the City of Lichfield, in February 1958. Another picture is an exterior view of the Enquiry Office and Travel Bureau in Bore Street. In the same issue Mr. J.W. Comelio wrote "It was with great regret that we learned of the sudden death of Mr. F.A. Kerrison who was Traffic Superintendent at Sutton Coldfield Garage up to 1954, when he had to retire due to ill-health". Bus fan Roger F. DE. Boer spoke of an interest in "the latter half of the 'fifties' in buses especially the Midland Red because it was rare to see those red vehicles amongst the blue and cream Birmingham Corporation buses passing the front door in Northfield". With Christopher Leigh "we would ride our pedal bicycles in search of the buses and Sutton Coldfield was the second Midland Red garage visited by me. When we rode past the 'Royal Town of Sutton Coldfield' sign our spirits were raised. It is likely that the visit to Sutton Coldfield took place on a Sunday, the traffic being less busy in those days on that day. By 1959 a strange bus was also found garaged at Sutton, CGJ 188, an ex-London Transport AEC Q' type used by Sutton Coldfield Old Peoples Welfare Committee, in grey/orange livery".

Annual sports day achievements

In 1958, Miss Betty Heaps, a qualified children's nurse, employed as a clerical officer at Sutton garage, took part in the Miss Midland Red Competition as Miss Sutton Coldfield, gained second place, at the Annual Sports Day in Bearwood. At the same event, three other unnamed office staff at Sutton garage won the 'egg and spoon', 'sack race' and 'potato race' events, with Mr. A. Shaw, a Sutton garage hand obtaining a special prize in the Hobbies, Arts and Crafts Competition. A further success for the company was achieved on 2nd November, 1959, as explained in Vol 2 of Midland Red p.6, "when the country's first motorway express coach, a vehicle specially designed by BMMO for the purpose, set off on its 80 m.p.h. trip down the M.l. to London. As more motorways were opened, further new services were developed and some existing long- distance routes diverted via the motorways to speed up their journeys". The initial London fares being 13/3 single and 21/3 for a return journey. Towards the end of 1959 Lichfield garage was pleased to have the allocation of an old Guy saloon, with a new fleet number of her own - 4843, who had "certainly won herself a place in the hearts of the junior school children". With Lichfield's gain, their correspondent Mr. F. Withers spoke of the city's loss with "Driver Webb being promoted to a higher rank at Sutton Garage. We now realize how much we depended on him as our club secretary. He was our founder and backbone, and Lichfield will be in his debt to him for a long time to come". The 14 year old son, Richard, of Mr. A.W.C. Turner, the Engineering Foreman at the Sutton Garage won the premier prize, competing against scholars at similar schools all over the country, involved devising a project of the competitor's won choice, within a certain range ... the prize in April, 1960 included a 12-day visit to Central Africa by "Comet-4 plane, as a guest of the Rhodesian Government".

Vehicle hire from Flights and Baxter

In the June 1960 Staff Bulletin, the General Manager, Mr. D.M. Sinclair, C.B.E., spoke of the company's continued staff shortage. "Sometimes the shortage has been worse than at other times. At the moment it is more serious than ever before, despite the recently introduced improvement in earnings and improved conditions to take effect next month". David Jenkins recalled that in the 1960s Flights provided Midland Red with up to "10 vehicles a day for peak service work with office staff and others used as conductors. At times the conductor stayed on the Parade or at some other heavy loading point and issued the tickets, the coach then operated non-stop to the city. This one person could deal with many hired vehicles". A transport contractor in the Chelmsley Wood area, Mr. Baxter, "hired 12/14 vehicles each day to the Midland Red. This hiring of vehicles was of course a very expensive operation for the BMMO". David said "Flights was a very good operator, vehicles and drivers were excellent". Mr. Keeley considered the Baxter coach hiring could not have been until 1967 when Chelmsley Wood began to be built. Malcolm advised me "I don't recall Baxter at all!" Yet around the same time Driver Walter E. Bond of Tamworth garage completed 40 years service, similar to his Conductor colleague at the same garage, Mr. William H. Foster, showing that some Midland Red staff had given long, reliable service to the company. Another 40 years servant from Tamworth was that Garage's Traffic Superintendent, Mr. Harry A. Brown, who started in August, 1920. For some twenty years he served as a special constable in the town. Over at Sutton garage, Mr. Comelio reported their Ladies Darts Team finished second in the league. Mrs. Johnson had the highest score, that of 147 in the final match.

BMMO's engineering prominence reduced

The press were introduced in September 1960 to the new Midland Red D 10 believed to be the "first double-decker in the world with an underfloor engine ... we can congratulate ourselves that those responsible for Midland Red 'blood-stock' seem to have 'bred' another 'winner' in the BMMO 'stables', of which we may expect to hear exciting news later!" Writing with the help of hindsight, Malcolm Keeley commented, "Only two were built which brought to an end the engineering prominence of the company. Midland Red continued to build a diminishing number of its own buses until 1971 but the designs were orthodox. The desperate shortage of engineering staff, tempted away by car factory wages, led to the end of production, with all future buses being built by outside manufacturers". Around the time of the D 10 introduction, the Sutton garage's club had been "completely reorganised, with the installation of a new bar and store-room, and also the removal of the stage, allowing greater freedom of movement". Drivers from the BMMO garages at Lichfield, Sutton and Tamworth probably identified with Mr. Sinclair's anger over the "inconsiderate parking of cars, particularly near road junctions, and poor lane discipline, which contributed greatly to congestion" for Midland Red crews in an around Birmingham. He went on "Although the discussions to which I refer apply particularly to the Birmingham area, the same difficulties exist, of course., in many other cities and towns where we operate". One of the contributors to the book, Mr. R. Coleman is seen in an April, 1961 issue of the Staff Bulletin, at the Sutton Garage's Fishing Club Dinner. Guests included Mr. and Mrs. J.W. Comelio, Mr. and Mrs. N.L. Cole and Mr. A.G.C. Baker. Mr. Coleman, the Chairman, presided over the prize giving. Mr. H. Allen presented the prizes, including the 'best catch of the season' to Mr. A. Littlewood.

BMMO murder

Probably the most distressing incident that Sutton Garage staff experienced was that recalled by Acting Inspector Tom Carey from June, 1961. "I was on duty the morning after Driver O'Neill murdered Garage Telephonist Eileen Harris. Mr. Comelio came in at approximately 0500 accompanied by 2 senior police officers. They went into his office and

On a misty day, S72 customers appeared to be pleased to board the S8 from Springfield Road, Falcon Lodge, to Sutton.
(M. Gottschalk)

A further view of Walsall fleet no.841, 841 FDH showing the Old Sutton Baptist church, now part of the MacDonald Restaurant site. (M. Gottschalk)

remained about an hour. I was curious to know what had happened. Later he informed me she had broken off her relationship with O'Neill and he had taken her out to a country lane near Shifnal and he had strangled her. At his trial he pleaded guilty and it was dealt with in record time". The Sutton Coldfield News of Friday June 9th gave further details. Mr. Comelio, in his monthly news report in the Staff Bulletin wrote "All employees at Sutton Garage would like to express their sincerest sympathies to the parents of Miss Eileen Harris on the tragic loss of their daughter, who was employed at Sutton Garage as Enquiry Clerk/Telephone Operator". The staff news obituary column announced "On the 2nd June - Miss E.J.M. Harris, Enquiry Clerk/Telephonist, Sutton Garage. Miss Harris was 18 years of age at the time of her tragic death and had completed 3 years' [broken] service with the company".

Lichfield MR top safety garage

A happier account came from Lichfield Garage correspondent Mr F. Withers who in the July/August 1961 Staff Bulletin Blew the Lichfield trumpet loudly with "This month's letter comes from the 'biggest-headed' bunch of Drivers on the Company; not without good cause, as Lichfield, for the first time ever, has 'topped the poll' with 31,400 miles per accident in the three months April, May and June 1961. It certainly is something to be proud of. The most praise must certainly go to the latest additions to the Driving

staff, as these have done their share towards this achievement with very little experience. Congratulations must also go to the 'Guards'.. for without the keen conscientious way that they blast their whistles on reversing we are sure we Drivers could manage to hit something!" The Birmingham "Evening Despatch" headline of 'J.P.s Praise Busman who helped a P.C.' referred to Sutton bus driver Eugene J. Harrington. The paper reported "A Midland Red bus driver was praised by a Sutton Coldfield magistrate today for going to the aid of a police officer who was arresting one of a number of youths for being drunk and disorderly". The Chairman of the bench, Alderman H.H. Turner said Driver Harrington "acted in the interests of the public". Eugene sustained an injury during the arrest. Miss Rose Farmer, who worked as a seasonal member of the Sutton Parade Enquiry Office team between 1934-36, later becoming the Chart-Room Supervisor at Spencer House, Disbeth, is seen in a mid 1930s picture of the front of the local office reproduced in the September 1961, Staff News. Miss Farmer, whose father operated a haulage contracting business in the town, is seen with Traffic Inspector Tucker, who retired in 1942 after 40 years service, Mr. Tucker's daughter, later to become Mrs. Evans, and Parcels-Boy, John Kennett. Incidentally, it was Inspector Tucker who received complaints from Sutton passengers, that the Red should be operating double-deck services. The Sutton garage opened in 1934, where he was resident Inspector.

Approval of D 9s

Lichfield correspondent Mr. F. Withers handed a pat-on-the-back "to the designers and builders of the D.9. This may sound a little late - in November 1961 - but Lichfield has only recently had the opportunity of using these new vehicles, and those belonged to Sutton; still we have the promise of two of our own, for early December". Mr. Withers may have been aware that 100 D.9 double-deck omnibuses and 100 single deck omnibuses were under construction in the Company's Central Works at the beginning of January, 1962, plus a further substantial rolling stock replacement programme of another 600 omnibuses. Of the 600, 150 would be D.9 type DDs, 300 S-16 SDs, then 100 Leyland "Leopard" SDS, and 50 Daimler "Fleetline" DDs. In addition, the BMMO Board had approved in the £3½ millions programme, "new modern bodies for the whole of the coach cruise fleet" in readiness for the 1963 Coach Cruise season.

Sutton's engineering staff had what could have been an impossible search. A Streetly passenger lost an eighth of an inch diamond from a three-stone ring on a bus, the number she recalled. She told the Birmingham Mail "I knew that it would only look like a tiny piece of glass, but no-one made any comment when I phoned the depot at Sutton Coldfield, and said I thought it had come out on the bus; and when I rang next day they calmly said 'yes', they had found my stone. It was a miracle. I'll never criticise a bus service again!" In early 1961, Sutton and Tamworth both had 40 year service award winners, with Mr. T. Brammer, Traffic Inspector at Tamworth, where he started on 13th February, 1922 as a Conductor, and Mr. Norman L. Cole the Engineering Superintendent at Sutton, who like Mr. Brammer, began at the former Twogates site, as a "greaser",

Walsall Corporation OLD 603, was an ex-London Transport RTL, seen in Victoria Road in 1960. (M. Gottschalk)

which started him on the lowest rung of the career ladder, on January 3rd 1922.

BMMOs fragile financial performance

Reading of the loyalty of Messers Brammer and Cole, with the perseverance of Sutton's bus cleaning team, and the £3½ million pound BMMO Board investment in its future bus and coach fleet, the casual reader could be forgiven in believing all was well for the company's immediate and long term future. The General Manager painted a different picture in his 3 page paper on One- Man Bus Operation of the 28th December, 1961. Mr. Sinclair was taking to task the Unions and some staff over their reluctance to increase the number of such Midland Red operations from its current 2.57% on stage carriage services. Many other operators were operating up to and over 20% of their mileage with one-man buses. The fragility of the company's financial performance was spelt out with:

a] 71.81% of the stage carriage services ran at a loss, many at a very heavy loss

b] Even with a high proportion of one-man operations, many would still be run at a loss. However., the GM forecast such amended operations would enable the company to keep operating those services.

c] The annual traffic was falling, in the last year they carried 12,915,198 few passengers, nearly 4% on stage carriage services, than the previous year.

d] In that last year costs had increased by 7.45%. Considering such poor figures for 1960, one wonders how

risky was the Board's £3½ million investment. To conclude Mr. Sinclair guaranteed there would be no redundancy as a

The Leyland PD2, ODH 804 is on the next Walsall via Little Aston and Aldridge, in April, 1963. (M. Gottschalk)

result of OMOs. Responding to my observations on the Board's £3½ million investment, Mr. Keeley pointed out "There had been a tremendous amount of vehicle buying in 1946-50 and these needed to be replaced". Malcolm thought 15 years was a typical life for a bus. "The new buses were generally 20% bigger and thus could carry more at no extra cost". Cliff Griffin's 1962 allocation list for the local garages was:

	Coach	Saloon	DD	Total
SN	1	16	54	71
TH	1	28	15	44
LD	3	11	6	20
DH	12	32	59	103

Mrs Margot McGrail, the Honorary Secretary of the Bus Committee, of Sutton's Old People's Welfare Committee wrote to Mr. Comelio "My Committee have asked me to express to you our sincere appreciation of the help given by your Company in the arrangements for the Old Folks Bus during its recent tour of outings. We would specially like to thank Mr. Cole for his work on the mechanical side, the cleaners who maintain the bus in such immaculate condition, your good self for arranging for a driver and, of course, Driver Milward himself, who gives such willing and friendly help in driving, and escorting the more infirm passengers".

Chapter Seven

Death and retirement of MR management

Death of Mr Wyndham Shire

Staff Bulletin editor Mr. W.H. Pine wrote the obituary of L.G. Wyndham Shire who died on 29th January, 1963, well over twenty years since his retirement. Mr. Pine penned "The name of Wyndham Shire is inextricably woven into the first three-and-a- half decades of the Midland Red story; and to him must be given the credit, very largely, for the fact that this company is unique amongst Omnibus operators in the country, in that it has been building its own fleet since 1924 or thereabouts. The light high-compression-engined single-decker he then designed and produced, and which he styled 'S.O.S' was his 'brain-child', and a child which developed in succeeding years and brought forth a very numerous progeny". As may be expected reference was made to Mr. Shire's active Midland Red involvement since 1912 and his working with the late 0. Cecil Power, "who died in harness in October, 1943". The arrival of the Beeching plan for the future of British Railways led the GM to advise Midland Red staff "All I can say at the moment is that, as a company which exists to provide a public service, we will be ready and willing to do all that is reasonable and practicable to meet the travelling needs of the public throughout the area which we serve".

Drivers' antics

Our focus comes back to the local garages with Sutton Coldfield in particular. Tom Carey pointing out that Driver Coleman was known for always singing in his cab. Taken up with his whistling, Tom recalled that on a 111 service, Ron "should have turned into Sutton Oak Road, at the Parson and Clerk Pub, but carried on along Chester Road, when he eventually was stopped by the conductor. Unable to reverse back along Chester Road due to traffic, he instead turned into the pub car park and came out into the Sutton Oak Road". Tom wondered "if the pub drinkers who had a few too many decided it was time to take the pledge when the Double Deck bus passed inches from the windows". A favourite joke of drivers Rose and Robinson was to "walk into the toilets and shout 'are you there Sid or Len'. Everybody in the toilets cowered down and shouted 'no, no,

This February 1962 picture in South Parade catches a brand new West Bromwich Corporation Damiler CVG 6 outside Chambers, with the Lawn Mower repair centre at the end of the Empress cinema car park. (M. Gottschalk)

A Guy Arab from Kemp and Shaw of Leicester at Sutton garage in June 1960. FJF90 was scrapped in March, 1962.
(M. Gottschalk)

no', because often a cup of cold water would come over the top". Inspector Jack Webster could not believe his eyes whilst standing in a shop doorway at Beggars Bush. "Three 107 buses" Tom retells "came along together. One followed the other around the island, 3 times! Conductor Watkins on the last bus saw the Inspector take off his hat and threw it on the ground, in disgust at their behaviour". Mr. Keeley thought that "Due to staff shortages discipline became weak because crews knew the company would have difficulty replacing them". Ray Jennings commenting on Mr. Webster said, "A fair inspector, but he turned up everywhere! " Ray found "it was a very good atmosphere at Sutton Garage, more like service life". However, Ray considered Mr. Tunnicliffe was a disciplinarian. Standing before him was like standing before a schoolmaster". Referring back to Inspector Webster, his son in Yorkshire, Dr. Roger Webster, told me when his father "put the uniform on it made him feel 6' tall". He also looked very smart. Apparently Jack was the Sutton Garage cricket and football team captain for a while. A kindly gesture of Inspector Webster was to wait for the children coming out of school then with the cricket team whisk them away by company transport to play at such venues as Swadlincote or Worcester on summer evenings. One of the attractions to the starving children was a splendid tea. Roger said with a chuckle in his voice, that "much to his mother's dismay, when father captained the Sutton Garage team at their home pitch in Rectory Park he kept his trousers up with an old tie! " Dr. Webster added "The team won cups under father's leadership". Because of the Inspector's sporting interests with the Garage he knew many famous people such as Danny Blanchflower and Joe Mercer. Danny gave Jack a pair of football semi-final tickets and when the Inspector delivered a parcel to Joe, he again came away with

complimentary tickets!

Scottish cruise engineering back-up

An interesting insight into the backroom support of the 7 and 14 day coach tours, that used Sutton stock is shared by John Wem. "2 coaches were kept special for 7 and 14 day trips. Scottish cruises usually went out on Saturday and returned on a Friday evening. One man usually worked overtime to inspect the coach and general services, adjust brakes etc., reline if necessary, oil change, grease up, check seats and interior, lights etc., tyres checked and road test by Assistant Foreman. The night cleaners cleaned, polished and vacuumed seats and carpets. A selected number of drivers drove the cruise coaches: John Hadwen, Eric Beck, Tom Orten, A. Steward and E. Blunden. If a cruise driver was in trouble with his coach, he tried to get to the overnight stay hotel. He always had to phone the Garage to notify us". Following passengers complaints that hired coaches from Scottish companies were often old and dirty, the Midland Red sent their own replacement vehicle to the stranded customers. "In the 1960s". John continued, "my first Scottish trip was to Lossiemouth in North East Scotland. Driver E. Beck came with me. We started at 2 p.m. on Thursday and arrived at the hotel at 5 p.m. Friday. The tour coach 4236 had a water leak, which caused a temporary seizure. Scottish & National Coaches had changed a hose but the engine was smoking so we drove the coach back slowly, taking it in turns to drive. We left Driver Hadwen with substitute 4237 and he continued his cruise with everyone happy". One Saturday evening Mr. Wem had a telephone call from Divisional Engineer Roger Harman requesting him to go to the aid of a Digbeth driver with a private party on the way

There were only about 10 of these Commer/Harrington "Contender" vehicles and Reddicroft owned two including JFV 527, seen in Railway Road in September 1961. It was sold to Don Everall in April, 1963, the month Reddicroft ceased trading. (M. Gottschalk)

to Nairn, currently at Peebles. With Garage Hand John Britten they collected 6 pistons, 6 cylinder liners, 2 cylinder heads, gaskets, oil, injectors and liner extractors from the Carlyle Works at Edgbaston, before taking an old coach, the only one available, from the Bearwood Garage. After a 7½ hours drive through the night, they worked on the broken down coach at a Peebles garage. "John took the top off the engine, while I worked at the bottom. By 2.00 p.m. we had changed the pistons and liners, cylinder heads and rebuilt the engine". As instructed they delivered the repaired vehicle to the driver at Nairn, arriving at 11.30 p.m. They found the driver in a party. "When we went in all the passengers cheered to get their nice coach back. So we joined the party while the driver arranged a room for us". The two Johns left on the Monday morning, taking turns at driving every hour, arriving back at 1.15 a.m. on Tuesday. Their commitment in getting the coach repaired showed the company's practice of providing the best back-up service for the tour drivers, though at times, a new vehicle was not available. Mr. Sinclair's monthly grouse in the May 1963 Staff Bulletin, about a "number of letters from the public complaining of early running on some of our services" reminded me of one of Conductor Colin Griffin's stories. "The silliest cause of a driver being called up to the office" he complained "Was a complaint from a passenger who said that the bus had left one minute early. The union man asked everyone present to check their watches. They did, and found that there was about a 3 minute range in the time. Case dismissed". In fairness to the GM, he argued that early running resulted in

much annoyance amongst passengers, "and even driving people to consider alternative means of transport".

Effective management policies

Reflecting on his service with the Company, David Jenkins considered Mr. Fytche as one of the most influential and effective managers the BMMO employed. David wrote, "The arrival of Mr. D.L. Fytche as Traffic Manager saved the company [my opinion]. We could not meet our operating costs, fare increases seldom reached the target set. One every year, two in one year. Many reasons for the vulnerable services. Top heavy in office staff. He reduced HQ staff, a whole department was eliminated". (Staff Dept.). "He forced out the Monday to Friday week - with Saturday and Sunday, rest day work. No overtime rate Monday to Friday. Saturday flat rate and Sunday time and a half. No difficulties after the battle to introduce, all mileage operated - less staff required. The consolidated wage rate was also introduced at the same time. All extraneous payment discontinued and incorporated into basic rate. This improved the basic rate by about 3 shillings per hour. It had the right result - staff stayed. The 35% of staff turnover ceased. In fact we soon had a waiting list". Malcolm was of the opinion that passengers on Monday to Friday BMMO services had an adequate service, however, "Saturday and Sunday travel by some Midland Red garages became a lottery". To run the services over the weekends, staff had to work their rest days. He thought "There were generally sufficient volunteers during daytime but evenings saw use of part-timers, and sadly, too many cancellations.

Despite this, I agree the action", [taken by Mr. Fytchel "was a sound one to protect its core business at that time". Driver T. Smith [No. 3] from the Upper Holland Road garage was complimented by a passenger for some smart footwork. "I had gone from Cannock to Sutton Coldfield on the 104, and being in a hurry to get to Birmingham, I got off the 104 and caught the 10.23 p.m., 107. I then realised I had left my parcel on the 104. I happened to mention it aloud, but by this time the 104 had turned round, so the driver of the 107 dashed across the road and retrieved my parcel for me. In these days of couldn't care less and 'I'm all right, Jack' it certainly stands out when someone puts themselves out to do a good turn, and as people are only too willing to write letters of complaint I feel that a letter of praise might be in order". The Sutton Garage children's outing on August 18th, 1963, saw 130 children enjoying the visit to Stourport, including a river trip. There was a sumptuous tea, with races and games organised by Drivers Coleman and Wozencroft. Conductor 'Nobby' Clark was the race judge. On Friday, November 1st, the Company's new Birmingham Bus Station was opened by the Lord Mayor of Birmingham, Alderman Doctor Louis Glass, J.P. The first service that left was 2986 HA a double-decker on the X72 route to Gloucester via Worcester. Another early service was an X99 via Sutton and Tamworth to Nottingham.

Lichfield garage answers to passenger questions

Some of the Lichfield Garage staff noted a selection of questions they had been asked at Lichfield Bus Station and some of the answers they had given, usually of a frivolous nature!

Q. Where does the Burton bus start from?
A. Birmingham
Q. How long will the next 765 be?
A. 36 feet
Q. Where is the Birmingham bus?
A. [After consulting watch] Shenstone. Presumably that meant it had already gone,
Q. What is the difference between this and a motorway coach?
A. Toilet is at the other end
Q. What time is the first bus to Stafford?
A. It went years ago.

The news item continued "No wonder Inspectors get ulcers trying to unravel that lot; but think of the confusion if Inspectors gave answers like it; however, they are bound by a 'badge' to tell the truth and nothing but the truth". Spring 1964 brought another Sutton and Lichfield tie up, Conductor Eddie Yates an import from the Royal town, marrying his ex-boss ' s daughter, Rose Innes. Traffic Superintendent 'Timetable' Smith was also congratulated. On the sad side, Mr. N. Cole died in May, 1964, the Garage Engineering Superintendent, at Sutton Coldfield, he was $62\frac{1}{2}$ years old, completing $42\frac{1}{4}$ years service with the company.

Sutton conductor's TV win

A Sutton Conductor appearing on the 'Take Your Pick' ITV programme, hosted by Michael Miles answered the three questions correctly. From the choice of boxes 4 or 13, Mr. Humphreys chose box 13 and won a trip to the World Fair in New York. The trip covered four days including meeting V.I.Ps in London and New York. A month later a second outing to the Wembley Studios was organised again, by Conductor T. Watkins, that time Driver Partlow encouraged by his mate's fortune, tried. He won a pair of Michael Miles' braces! Walsall Transport provided a Lichfield bus replacement service with the closure of the Burton-on-Trent to Wolverhampton High Level train service on the 18th

In July 1962, Barratts the Radio and TV shop still operated on the corner of Station Street and Mill Street, when prototype Midland Red S16, 5095 HA, was on its first day in revenue earning service. (M. Gottschalk)

Eagle eyed readers will note these two S13 type buses have slightly different bodies as they wait for their duties in January 1962 at Sutton garage. (M. Gottschalk)

January, 1965. The two through services from Lichfield to Wolverhampton left at 6.45 a.m. and .7.45 a.m., with a return bus leaving from Wolverhampton at 4.30 p.m. The Ministry of Transport considered the needs of the travelling public would be met by the three bus journeys. I am not sure how long the service remained financially viable and when it ceased. A quite different Midland Red service a month later that had proved to be successful, notched up its millionth passenger, a Miss Marilyn Harrison, on 19th February, since the M.E.I. motorway service to London began on 2nd November, 1959. Mr. D. L. Fytche, Traffic Manager, earlier spoken of by David Jenkins, presented a leather suitcase to the surprised and delighted passenger, a teacher at Bournville Grammar School. The Company's coaches covered 4,114,000 miles in the $5\frac{1}{4}$ years of the M.E.I. service. Although those official M.E.I. figures brought the GM satisfaction, data from the MOT was more likely to have given him a severe headache.

Increase of non public transport vehicles continues

"More and more people, in their hundreds of thousands", Mr. Sinclair informed his staff in the Spring of 1965, "are acquiring private cars - and more and more people will do so, especially when public transport becomes unreliable, and at times non-existent". He was referring to the last 3 months of 1964. Nearly $12\frac{1}{2}$ million vehicles of all kinds were on Great Britain's roads. That was an increase of 923,000 vehicles - an 8% increase over the same period the previous year. During that time only 1,000 more passenger vehicles were used.
Frank Withers at Lichfield, never one to miss the chance to stir the muck, told Bulletin readers that the Three Spires

Garage had gained another main road turn from Sutton. Tamworth, Mr. Withers wrote, turned it down because "it was too hard for them. So it has been passed on to us". One wonders if Frank knew when to stop leg pulling because he went on to say "The Union are pushing for a notice to be put up at Sutton, stating that it is under 'New Management'". Presumably from Trent Valley Road, Lichfield. John 'Abdul' Allison caused consternation for some Lichfield mothers. "John went to the aid of a lady passenger on his bus, who had with her five small children. He gently handed down the toddlers to the lady". As he stepped back on the vehicle an "irate lady demanded her child back! After a rapid recount, he found that six, and not five had left his loving care!" Tamworth garage in November 1965 saw the departure of its longest serving conductor and driver into retirement. Driver Walter E. Bond after $45\frac{1}{2}$ years service and Conductor J. Edgar Bramall, who spent all his $46\frac{1}{2}$ years company service at Tamworth. Edgar left as the BMMO's longest-serving Conductor. Over at Sutton Garage, I was reminded by David Jenkins of Mr. R. Harman's promotion from Garage Engineering superintendent to Divisional Engineer of the Birmingham District. Mr. J.W. Womar, General Manager of The Potteries Motor Traction Company Ltd. became the Midland Red Deputy General Manager on 1st March, 1966. Mr. Sinclair was due to retire at the end of the year. A new addition to the Lichfield fleet early in 1966 was considered by some of the staff as probably "the finest stage carriage bus in Britain", however it was thought 5723 would be improved by the addition "of a luggage boot adding the finishing touch to what must be the bus of tomorrow". According to Messrs Gray, Keeley and Seale it was one of a group of three denoted as S21A, DHA 722-4C. Two new Lichfield drivers began for the 1966 cruise season, Stan Fellows and Harry Yates. Mr. Withers commented for them it could be "a season of trial and error, and something to look back on and laugh about later. There will be times this season, however, when they will not feel like laughing at all". In July, Frank mentioned that some of the overspill staff from Birmingham were enlarging their families but they were welcome including the son of Mr. and Mrs. "Alex" Thomas.

Sutton Waybill counter summary examples from Mr Colin Griffin

Cliff Griffin helpfully submitted two specimen waybill counter summaries and related journey waybills for two shifts in July, 1966. He named his drivers as C. Beck and E. Blunden, both Upper Holland Road staff. The main road services tend to be 105 dominated with a late 108 trip, whilst the week later duties stay with the up and down sequence of S71s. Cliff advised me that the Sutton routes had nick-names to identify them. These were:

S63/73 the Boldmere Flyer
S67/76 the Bush Swinger

All routes from Birmingham to Sutton via Wylde Green were the Main Road; 107s were called Oscotts; 113 was the Hardwick; 114 was the Falcon. Many turns included a 114 to town [Birmingham], 113 to and from Streetly, then 114 to Sutton, and this was called a round trip. 175 [in later days renumbered as the 166] was the Track - so called because it was a very busy, and thus very fast route. When you had 3

trips on the Track you didn't want any extra!" Cliff shares some stories from Sutton Coldfield Garage which happened in the 1960s and 1970s when he was a conductor at Upper Holland Road. Driver Alf Smith was known as "Pedro" because of his Mexican style moustache. He was small of stature and considered to be an excellent driver. "A passenger came downstairs on the double deck OMO, looking a little pale. When Alf asked if he was alright, the passenger explained that he had been on the front seat when the bus had gone under a particularly narrow bridge at speed. "I really didn't think that you could get through there, mate", he said. "You should do what I do if it worries you", replied Alf. Rather unwisely, the passenger enquired what that was, only to be told, "If the gap looks too narrow, I just shut my eyes!"

Alf's relationship with "Checkers [Inspectors] was always a bit strained", Cliff told me. "He was known to have been giving his passengers a reasonably smooth ride until a checker got on. Then thrown everyone around like mad until the checker got off. At this point, he would revert to the smooth ride. This worked, as some checkers would avoid his bus if they could". My favourite story of Pedro is the one about the D 9 half cab, as he drove along Colmore Row. "Glancing into the interior mirror", Cliff informed me, "he could see no-one was looking, so he huddled down into the seat, opened the cab door and then slammed it. Everyone looked up to see an apparently empty cab while the bus hurtled towards the hairpin bend by the Town Hall!

4953 is filling up for the 114 Sutton Coldfield - Birmingham via Falcon Lodge service, adjacent to the Empress Cinema, in South Parade. (M. Gottschalk)

At the last minute he put them out of their misery by sitting up again". The last Cliff heard was that Pedro was "the record holder for the fastest time on the last 107 out of Birmingham. This left the Bus Station at 0015 hours, and was due in Garage at 0100. Alf was known to do it in 17 minutes, and I have seen him take the islands in College Road without slowing down enough to change down from top!"

Sutton garage staff stories

Cliff pointed out to me that the Company used to differentiate between two or more of the same surname by numbering them. "For example" Cliff went on "there were about 5 Jones's and two Griffiths's - Vic and Ron". His main untypical memory of Vic was on the last X12 from Derby of the day, in pre-Spaghetti days, near the bottom of Gravelly Hill. Cliff "felt a bump as the bus slowed for the lights. I looked down the vehicle, thinking that a case had fallen from the luggage racks, but could see nothing. We next became aware of someone waving at us from the pavement, telling us that we had run someone over. What had happened was that a drunk was in such a bad state that the rush of wind from the passing bus had been enough to put him off balance, and he had fallen under the back wheel. Needless to say, he was dead. By the time we had finished the paper-work at Erdington police station, it was about 0200 hours, the next day". Vic's brother, Griffiths 2, Ron, for some unknown reason called Rabbit, "was famous for his dislike of 'Corpo' passengers [Birmingham Corporation Transport passengers], and any runners within the city boundary were either very fast or very disappointed if it was

his bus they were running for!" Conductor Frank Thorne witnessed the creation of two buses from one, when the 103 was returning from Roughley to the garage. Cliff tells us "On this occasion they took a short cut, when the bus was officially in service, down Little Sutton Lane. This was an unfortunate choice by the driver [who was relatively new to the job] as they had a decker and there is a low bridge under the railway. The inevitable happened!" Cliff was on a 107 [Oscotts] service, driven by Johnny Davies "when he suddenly screeched to a halt at Perry Barr Station. On going out to see what the problem was, he told me that the bananas at the shop we had just passed were very cheap - did I want any?!" Alf Smith was not the only one to play up the passengers on occasions. There was the "driver who pretended to be nearly blind, allowing his conductor to help him across the bus station, onto the bus and into the cab". A further wind-up "was of a driver and conductor who 'changed places' when they got to the bus, because the 'conductor wanted to have a go at driving'. Having received instructions from his mate what the pedals were for and how it worked, off he went". The passengers were not "informed that both crew had both badges!" As a schoolboy Cliff thought driver Ron Coleman reminded him and other Riland Bedford scholars of a nationally known TV character at the time. "The heavy features and permanent pipe in the mouth reminded us of the title character in the Maigret TV programme that was popular at the time".

Mill Street Car Park was a venue where Midland Red luxury coaches were open to Public inspection with a view to gaining patronage. (M. Gottschalk)

Chapter Eight

Midland Red nationalised, and Lichfield closure

Review of early Sutton services

A three part article in 1967 Staff Bulletins on the first Midland Red Timetable develops the data given by Peter Hale of the Omnibus Society under our earlier heading, Review of Midland Red Sutton Services: 1913-1928.

In Alec.G. Jenson's 1967 article he says that "Sutton Coldfield was served by buses operated by the Birmingham Omnibus Conveyance Co. in 1837 and in the 1850s by buses operating from various hotels in Bull Street/High Street, Birmingham and by William Sheppard who was a well known bus operator, from the Swan, New Street. He is recorded as operating in 1853 and until 1862". The 1914 Midland Red Motor Services' map of 1914 shows the initial services No. 11, Chester Road, Sutton and Mere Green via Four Oaks and No. 12 Chester Road and Sutton via Boldmere Road, Chester Road and New Oscott [Beggars Bush]. Incidentally, the first Official Time Table was issued free in March, 1914. Copies were available in 'please take one' boxes on the buses. The April and May issues were free, but in June, 1914 the publication was taken over by The Tram Guides Co. and cost 1d. The No. 11 began during the week ending the 13th May, 1913 from Chester Road tram terminus from 6.30 a.m. It was a 30 minute service in the weekday mornings, increasing to a 15 minute interval service during the afternoon and evening until 10.30 p.m. to Sutton and every 30 minutes all day to Mere Green. The Sunday service at 30 minute intervals ran from noon to 2 p.m. followed by the weekday frequency until 10 p.m., and every 30 minutes to Mere Green. The "through fare was 2d to Sutton, 3d return, except on Sundays and Bank Holidays and 3½d through fare to Mere Green. The service is now incorporated in Nos 102, 103 and 108". Mr. Alec Jenson advised the Bulletin readers Service No. 12 began week ending 22nd August, 1913 from the Chester Road tram terminus. An hourly service began at 11.20 a.m. to Sutton on weekdays until 9.20 p.m.; 10.20 p.m. on Saturdays and from 2.20 p.m. on Sundays. The through fare was 2d to Sutton and a 3d return except on Sundays and Bank Holidays. Present service is No. S 73. The hourly weekday service to New Oscott ran hourly from 11.00 a.m. until 9 p.m. on weekdays, until 10 and 11 p.m. on Saturdays, and hourly from 2 p.m. until 10 p.m. on Sundays.

A long service cleaner

Frank ["Carlos"] Campagna, who wrote from Italy about his respect for Mr. 'Timetable' Smith, was travelling north along the A38 in an early winter 1967 fog. He decided to follow a bus. The bus stopped outside the Victoria Hospital, and Frank took the lead. "Whilst he was messing about trying to find the off-side lane, the bus soon caught up with him. It then happened that Frank turned too soon and ended up in the Bowling Green! - and yes - the bus followed him. The bus indicator blind had S.W. on it! A couple of months later, Sutton Coldfield Conductress Miss M. Ryan had completed 25 years service from the 19th February, 1943. Miss F. Gadsdon, an Enquiry Clerk at the Parade Office retired after 17½ years service and Hugh Mallin, a night cleaner at the garage who had 33 years service with the Company died after a short illness. Another of the Company's unsung heroes from the cleaning brigade was Mr. Joseph Taylor, who completed 40 years BMMO service from 26th July, 1928, initially at the Two Gates Garage, moving to the new Aldergate Garage that opened on 3rd August, 1928, with a capacity of 38 vehicles. Incidentally, the Two Gates Garage opened on 1st February, 1918, and closed after the new Garage opened. The BMMO company kept the Two Gates ex-North Warwickshire premises until the former firm ceased in 1947. Mr. Taylor transferred to Upper Holland Road Garage with the opening on 26th August, 1934 "and here he has remained ever since". Joseph spent all the 40 years on night shifts. He became the Chargehand Cleaner at Sutton. In his earlier years he played for Tamworth Garage football teams.

Midland Red Nationalised

"The controlling owners of BMMO, the British Electric Traction Co. Ltd," wrote Malcolm Keeley, "sold its share holdings in United Kingdom bus companies, to the Transport Holding Co, which was state-owned, with effect from 14/2/68. Midland Red was thus nationalised. The THC became the National Bus Company on 1/1/69". A letter from Mr. T.W.H. Gailey, CBE, the Chief Executive of the National Bus Company, confirmed these details in the January-February, 1969, Staff Bulletin "... But to all of us as we stand at the threshold of the new year it is time for taking a fresh look at things". "I trust, therefore., that you feel with me that the formation of the National Bus Company will herald a new era in road passenger transport in England and Wales. It provides us with an opportunity to improve upon an efficient and viable industry. Our aim is unchanged, to provide the best possible service to the public in an economical way. I know that I can count on your support". By the way, the Editor from July 1968, Mr. A.J. Bishop, began the bimonthly SB with the January- February issue. Some of John Wem's recollections of Sutton Garage staff includes Driver Bobby [Cracker] Burns with an appropriate bus movement. "Mr. Burns was, a very jovial man, good for a laugh", said John. "When we went out socially with parties, such as to Windsor many years ago, passengers wanted to go to the toilets, miles from anywhere. Men one side of the coach, women the other. Then he moved the bus

This Worcester Midland Red West Clock above the Travel shop is believed to have previously been at Sutton Coldfield. (M. Concannon)

away! Another driver, Jack Young, "had trouble with a speedo light in his cab. He came into the Garage, with a candle burning in the centre of the steering wheel!" Mr. Wem shared three sad memories. "Garage Hand Alex Zander, a refugee from Latvia, collapsed and died in a pit while changing an engine on a coach". John was sad to learn of Eileen's murder, speaking of John or Tony O'Neill, "He seemed a nice man, we just don't know what went wrong". Mr. Wem called to mind Driver Brian Shergold who having "worked a morning shift, went home, sat in a chair, and never woke up. He was only about 40 years of age or younger".

Massive recruitment campaign

Frank Withers told the story of an unnamed Lichfield Driver who "recently staggered out of bed feeling just a little bit thick, so he searched about in the bathroom for the Alka Seltzer, popped two Steradent tablets into a glass of water and drank them! It did not do his head much good but he came to work with a wonderful feeling of inner cleanliness!" Mr. Womar informed staff in the September-October 1969 SB, of the company's "massive recruitment campaign launched on 11th September, to coincide with the new and improved wage rates, in an attempt to attract entrants into our industry and persuade others who have left, to return, and thereby re-establish our standing in the eyes of the travelling public". In a threatening tone he went on "The only alternative if we are not successful will be a substantial cut in services., and this is the last thing we wish to do, for there is no future in it". More hopefully "It is already

encouraging that a number of additional staff have been engaged including several former employees". A 26 year old recruit was Colin Moss, now of the Tamworth Midland Red North depot, who joined at Sutton Garage, after driver training at Bearwood Training School. His test drive in 1969 was on CI 3311. Whilst route learning "on service 175 down a lane near Minworth, one regular lady passenger gave the crew and learner "who was sitting near the front of the single decker an apple each, -showing local human concern for the Midland Red staff". On one X12 Derby-Birmingham service, operated by Leyland Saloon 5847, "it carried 50 cycle frames. Each had to have a ticket stuck on it. Some frames went in the large boot, the remainder at the back of the bus, on seats and stacked on the floor". Mr. Moss thought the BMMO own built vehicles "would probably have become the most advanced in the world, a world leader". He gave an example of the MR home built, which were similar to the 1990 Volvo vehicles. "mr. Keeley interpreted Colin's description as the D/O underfloor engined double decker built 1960-1, a configuration not repeated in the UK until Volvo did a quarter of a century later".

A view from the kitchen

In 1969, Mrs. Eileen Keating moved as a Canteen Assistant from the Bull Ring Canteen to Sutton Garage. She was the Canteen Supervisor for a time, but did not tell everybody. A canteen service was maintained between 6 a.m. - 8 p.m. She recalled three main turns, 6 a.m. - 2 p.m.; 9 a.m. - 3 p.m.; and 2 - 8 p.m. Some of the washing up team she considered "were better than any washing machine, with one of the

Inspectors coming into the kitchen to test and see how clean the plates and cups were, We did not know when they were coming", Eileen added. "Irene, the cook, planned some lovely menus, such as cottage pie, braised steak, chicken portions, steak and kidney pie, fish cakes, fish and chips on Fridays. There was a variety of vegetables, rice pudding, bread pudding and bread and butter pudding. Lunches were served from noon - 3 p.m..." the Drivers, Conductors sat apart from the office staff". "The Garage Mechanics" she advised me, "had their own tables and were served over the counter. They were so dirty because of their work". "One factory, by the garage, without a canteen, had some of their staff coming to our side door with lunch orders. The idea of coming to the side door, rather than coming into the canteen with company staff, was to avoid jealousy". For the BMMOs early duty staff, sausages, bacon, tomato, etc were available until 11 a.m. Mrs. Keating remembers "Mr. Carmelo being a regular to come in for his breakfast. The next manager did not, as far as I recall". At one stage at Upper Holland Road Garage "tea was 5d, going up to 6d, 3d for a slice of toast, only $2\frac{1}{2}$d for a crust! We stocked all makes of pop. During the winter, we served soup every day". The "best time each year in the canteen, was Christmas. Two turkeys, Christmas puddings or mince tart, all made in the kitchen and brought in". Most of the BMMO staff enjoyed and appreciated the service provided by Irene, Jayne, Joan, Isobel, Alice, and others. Irene thought Sutton was a good place to work in. "In the early days", she told me. "they did not keep to hygiene rules, though later 'No Smoking' signs were erected".

The advertisement in the autumn of 1969, seeking to recruit more BMMO staff spoke of "21 days holiday with pay, free travel concessions, uniform provided, our own sports and social activities, a sick-pay scheme. Talking of pay, average duty week earnings are about £17, and if you're a one-man operative, it can be up to £3 a week extra. In addition there were ample opportunities for overtime which also push up total wages". A follow-up to the recruitment campaign was a series of specially arranged Buffet evenings for new staff or those rejoining the company in the last twelve months. The evenings were held between November 1969-April 1970. Pages 14-15 of the January- February 1970 Staff Bulletin had an article on "The Long 'Red Line'" a tribute to the 45 years or so that the BMMO had built its own vehicles, with the policy not to build any more after the completion of S23, UHA 941 H, fleet number 5941. This policy was referred to earlier by Mr. Malcolm Keeley. An accompanying photo to 5941 is of a S.O.S. of 1924, the first bus to be entirely designed and built by Midland Red. HA 2334 is shown with a Lichfield and Burton destination plate on the front. The Long Red Line article is continued on pp 12-13 of the March-April edition. The three last pictures are of a Leyland LS.20, and 'LC 9' coach with Panorama body styling by Plaxtons and a OMO Daimler 'fleetline', SHA 863 G, showing a D13 Birmingham via Wylde Green blind on the 'DD. 13'.

Recognition of management and union contributions

The importance of effective relationships between management and the union representatives was highlighted by articles on Industrial Relations teamwork and Management and Union Seminars in the November/December 1970 issue of the Staff Bulletin, one of the recently restyled magazines. A regular trade union column was added. The March/April 1971 Staff Bulletin gave

Staffordshire County Council Highways Department owned the former Lichfield Midland Red Garage in 1996 at the Trent Valley Island. A minibus is seen coming from the Boley Park Island. (M. Concannon)

the BMMO management viewpoint of the so-called WMPTE 'Take over' of the Midland Red which was causing so much anxiety amongst current staff in 1971 and returned MR staff. Readers were advised that "under the terms of the Transport Act 1968, a statutory obligation was placed on the National Bus Company [or its subsidiary - in this case, Midland Red] and the West Midlands P.T.E. 'to co-operate with one another in the reorganisation of bus services within, to and from the area and for that purpose to enter into agreements as to the services to be provided by the Company in or in connection with, that area and as to the terms on which those services are to be provided'". The NBC Board "decided that if Midland Red could regain its viability they would be happy for it to continue". Apparently a 1970 target of a £900,000 balance finished with a loss of nearly £700,000, a deterioration of over £1½m pounds. To regain viability the company had to "a] Reduce the intake of new vehicles b] Reduce or stop all building maintenance c] Close unremunerative garages d] Cease unremunerative routes e] Increase one-man operation quickly f] Revise services, schedules and working arrangements at all garages quickly g] Reduce administration and vehicle requirements and h] Reduce the labour force at all levels". In the process, the Statement continued "We must NOT reduce total revenue - in fact we must try and increase it, otherwise, in the short term there will be insufficient money coming in to pay our way". The staff at Lichfield noted point 7 with considerable alarm "Each garage, mostly rural, which has so far been losing money will be examined to see how the organisation and conditions can be altered to ensure at least a break even position". The closing paragraph spelt out the inevitable future for some Midland Red ventures. "The prescription now known as 'Operation Phoenix' may appear unpalatable as it does include garage closures and staff level reductions. However, the hard facts of life are, that we are providing

more services, with a bigger organisation, than the public or local authorities will support. Therefore, we must contract to a level where the costs are equivalent to the money which customers are prepared to pay for the service which they use. The alternative to this remedy could be the demise of Midland Red which is not conceivable but ought to be recognised". Some of the SB readers of that issue may have noted the item on page 7 to be an indication of what was to come. Last journey of service S67/76. Driver Colin Moss decided to record the last journey on film. It showed Conductress Mrs. M. Jeffers and Driver Keith Faulkner both of Lichfield Garage in front of 5130 at 10 p.m. at Six Ways. The news item concluded "This service was, for many years, operated by Sutton Garage, but due to an exchange of routes it was, in the latter stages, operated by crews from Lichfield".

3301 Preservation Society and Lichfield closure

News was given that 3301 had gone into honourable retirement after 336,000 miles. A photo on page 11 of the March/April Bulletin recorded 3301 leaving Bearwood, on February 19th. The 5 members of the MR team who had formed the 3301 Preservation Society were Traffic Inspector, B. Morris; Secretary, Driver L. Morgan; and Treasurer, Conductor C. Griffin, another of our contributors. The two other members were: Mr. D. Oughton and Mr. L. Watts of the Engineering Department. The Lichfield correspondent wrote of the Garage's hurt and anger over its proposed closure. The writer spoke of the garage's "body shop, engine shop and chassis steam cleaner, and all buses that are retired are done so through Lichfield. Having been stripped of all useful parts first. Take all this into consideration and tell us where is the economy in closing down the Lichfield depot?" The writer said Lichfield had worked O.M.O. buses on some

Mike Concannon found this Midland MacDonalds DD hard to locate. Seen outside the Tamworth Garage, in 1996.
(Mike Concannon)

KHA 301 - The 5 members of the MR team that formed the 3301 preservation Society, are: B.Morris; L.Morgan; C.Griffin (contributor to Wheels around Sutton); D.Oughton and L.Watts. (3301 Preservation Society)

routes for nearly three years. The garage was Company owned. An Editorial note was under the Lichfield contribution. "Note: Whilst the annoyance expressed by our correspondent is understandable in circumstances it must be pointed out that this Garage has been very unprofitable. The Company's policy of closing unprofitable garages has been tempered by the criterion of minimum dislocation of public services and minimum inconvenience to staff employed at those garages". The next SB showed Councillor Herbert Bourne, Chairman of Staffordshire County Council Roads and Bridges Committee, officially opening the new $3\frac{1}{2}$ miles Lichfield eastern by-pass, costing $£2\frac{3}{4}$m from Streethay to

The British Bus owners of Midland have maintenance facilities in the Tamworth garage, which over the years had connections with the Sutton and Lichfield Depots. (Mike Concannon)

Wall. At the Safe Driving Awards and Awards of Merit at the Belfry Hotel, WishaW, for staff from Lichfield, Sutton Coldfield, Tamworth and Digbeth, the General Manager, Mr. J.W. Womar, spoke about the end of the Garage cross subsidisation policy. He paid tribute to the Lichfield Garage Union Committee and the Committees of those garages who had co- operated so well in arranging transfer for those members of the team who wanted to go to other garages. "Mr. B. Sabell, Central Division Manager, Chairman for the evening, referred to the 'great sadness' that was in the air due to the closure of Lichfield Garage". Mr. Withers in the garage's last contribution advised those looking for staff that "At the Safe Driving Awards, Lichfield took top place out of the garages present, so all garages taking on drivers from Lichfield you must be getting good ones". In the same SB Tamworth "wished to convey their deepest regrets to our colleagues at Lichfield Garage". Another sad note was given in the May/June 1971 SB. It was announced that "the Midland Red's first General Manager, Mr. Donald Sinclair, died at the Queen Elizabeth Hospital, Birmingham, on June 17th, aged 69. The funeral took place on Wednesday, June 23rd, 1971, when there was a strong contingent of ex-colleagues from the Company and the industry paying their last respects". The Lichfield Mercury of 4th June stated that offers had been made for "the Midland Red garage following its closure last Friday". Black Friday was the heading of the half page article in the SB. It was a sad day on Friday, May 28th when both Lichfield and Cradley Heath Garages operated for the last time. By Saturday, May 29th, all vehicles had been transferred to other garages together with those supervisors and crews who were prepared to move with the buses and start a new era of service in different surroundings. The SB continued : "Alas there were some who did not choose to do this, and under the redundancy schemes left the Company's service. Lichfield Garage, a modern, purpose-built unit was opened on September 17th' 1954, but only managed to survive for $16\frac{1}{2}$ years. During that time the fleet hovered about the 20 mark, although there always seemed to be more because the spare land at the back was used as a dumping ground for obsolete buses awaiting their turn for sale, cannibalisation., or eventual transfer to the breaker's yard". On a happier note Mrs. Pauline Hand became Tamworth's first lady driver. "We understand" wrote the correspondent, "that on her first day behind the wheel, all traffic in Tamworth kept more to the left than usual. All joking apart, well done Pauline".

Chapter Nine

'Bright' and 'strong' MR future and Sutton garage closes

"When Lichfield Garage closed", John Wem informed me, "an EX/WD Ford Thames Breakdown vehicle was sent to Sutton for us to use when we had changed the engine. A V8 engine was bought. I fixed it after making many modifications to the exhaust etc., with the aid of Tony, one of the Garage Hands. The first trip was to London to tow a coach back with a broken crankshaft. We went via the A5. We found the breakdown vehicle sluggish on hills, and drinking petrol. We had to keep filling it up using bunkering cards. When we were travelling down Kilburn High Street in London, I pulled into the side and crawled under and wound some brake off in case they were binding. On the way back we had all sorts of trouble, engine overheating, petrol evaporating. It would not pull the coach more than 5 mph and cyclists were passing us. At midnight I phoned Mr. Harman and told him so he said leave the coach at Stoney Stratford United Counties Garage. We stayed the night and come back with the breakdown truck in the morning, arriving back at 2.00 pm, to a welcome of cheers as we entered the garage. Mr. Harman was not very happy. He wanted to know what we had done. Then he took the Breakdown Truck up Reddicap Hill and down Rectory Road". He said "I ought to give you a pat on the back to get to London and back. Not a kick up the pants!'" Further investigation proved the wrong engine had been installed. Not a 40hp but a 20hp. In the 36 hours London return trip the vehicle used 65 gallons of petrol!.

Sutton MR garage limited life span

The future of the Midland Red operations from the Sutton Garage in the Summer and Autumn of 1971 had a limited life span, as Peter Hale gives a survey of the Sutton services at 28th August, 1971. "Midland Red imposed several cuts in services during 1971, following a large trading loss in 1970. This list shows the 'after' position and was virtually unchanged when WMPTE took over on 3rd December, 1973. The 'before' list would have shown more services than the 1948 list.

Sutton Service list, 28th August, 1971

X12 Birmingham-Sutton-Lichfield-Burton-Derby
X99 Birmingham-Sutton-Tamworth-Nottingham
S62 Chester Road-Streetly-Sutton-Boldmere-Chester Road
S63 Chester Road-Boldmere-Sutton-Streetly-Chester Road
S65 Chester Road-Walmley-Sutton
S66 Sutton-Falcon Lodge
S71 Erdington-Walmley-Sutton Coldfield
S74 Sutton-Falcon Lodge-Wishaw
105 Birmingham-Chester Road-Walmley-Sutton
107 Birmingham-New Oscott-Sutton
110 Birmingham-Sutton-Tamworth

112 Birmingham-Sutton-Lichfield-Burton
113 Birmingham-New Oscott-Hardwicke Arms
114 Birmingham-Walmley-Falcon Lodge-Sutton
115 Walsall-Streetly-Sutton-New Oscott-Walsall
117 Walsall-New Oscott-Sutton-Streetly-Walsall
166 Sutton-Minworth-Chelmsley Wood-Solihull

To try and catch the continuing feelings of many staff with the eventual demise of MR operations at Sutton, a number of quotes are given. The SB of September/October 1971 had a cover black and white aerial picture of the "Spaghetti" interchange, news that the third MR garage, Wolverhampton, had closed. An article reported "Unfortunately, many of the staff found the distances involved in travelling to other garages too great and this deterred them from moving with the buses, therefore under the redundancy schemes, they have left the company's service". The twice enlarged Bromsgrove garage closed on 31st December, 1971.

BMMO breaks even

Mr. Womar informed staff that the company had stopped losing money and had reached a break even point. Two losses to the BMMO were the deaths of Dolly Spooner with 16 years broken service, a conductress at Tamworth, who had transferred when the Lichfield garage closed, and on 7th January, 1972, a day later, Mr. F.L. Bacchus, ex-Engineering Inspector, Central Division, who had completed 50 years service on his retirement in 1968. On the 1st February, Mr. J. Walter Womar the former Director and General Manager of the BMMO Co Ltd, took the newly created post of Executive Director for Property Development with the N.B.C. A N.B.C. management reorganisation placed the Midland Red in the Western Division. Mr. J.H. Gilbert from the 1st April, took over as General Manager of the MR, his last post was Director and General Manager of the East Kent Road Car Company Ltd., Mr. Gilbert died at the age of 53, on 4th August, during a holiday in Scotland, staying at a relative's farm on the Isle of Arran. 4 days before his death, Mr. Gilbert, his wife and 2 children., by chance met Driver Trevor Hale of Digbeth Garage, operating the inclusive tour 'The Far North'. "They had a chat while Driver Hale was awaiting his party".

A feature on 'Bus advertising is big business' shows 2 DD with advertising on, one for a greyhound stadium and the other encouraging people at a Berni Inn, had service 107 displayed, operating between Sutton via New Oscott. In the summer of 1972 the MR was currently displaying 4,500 exterior advertisements on its fleet. The SB spoke of another MR achievement on Wednesday, 24th May, "When the 'Spaghetti Junction' interchange was opened by the Rt. Hon. Peter Walker, M.P., after the official opening ceremony, once again Midland Red coaches were the first to travel over the junction, as was the case when the M1 was opened in 1959. We provided 12 coaches on a Private Hire contract". The N.B.C. started to emphasise its national identity, with the symbol appearing alongside the words Midland Red. The new General Manager of the BMMO Co Ltd., was Mr. Peter Brook. In addition, he was appointed Chief General Manager of the company, and that of two other Western Division companies.

Last MR Staff Bulletin

Issue 287 of the SB in December 1972 was the last one, going back to September, 1946. The Sutton correspondent wrote, "it is with regret that we learn that Staff Bulletin is being discontinued - in its present form. We would like to record the fact that it has been a means of keeping in touch with all the happenings within the company and its personalities". Of the 11 last Pats on the Back for MR staff, two went to Sutton personnel. Vic Griffiths, referred to by Mr. Griffin, was complimented for the help given on the Mull, Oban and Western Highlands tour. A husband and wife said "Quiet, but efficient, and always courteous, we would like you to know he contributed materially to our enjoyment of a most interesting tour". Driver Courier, Mr. R. Holland was also spoken of with high praise by a couple on a later Scottish tour "...and the services of the Driver are to be commended. Johnnie, the name we knew him by, was courteous, very considerate and most helpful, and in view of the fact that he was brought on this tour due to the illness of the regular driver, he is to be congratulated for his knowledge of the country., both geographically and historically". A young bus enthusiast at the time was Peter Organ, living in Sutton Coldfield. He told me "To me, Midland Red under its former guise of BMMO always held a fascination for me as a child because the individuality of its mainly self-built fleet gave it a 'class' which didn't exist under the likes of West Bromwich Corporation who ran into Sutton on the 25 service or Birmingham Corporation with its cheaper services that ran very firmly to the Birmingham/Sutton borders in those days ... From an early age the organisation of bus services has always been an interest to me and I often made my way to the garage to collect time tables from the garage's front office [before it transferred to Sutton Parade]. This was really only an excuse

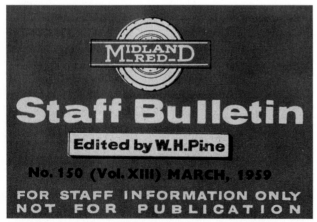

Midland red employees had their own staff Bulletin for 26 years. A considerable amount of information from the Bulletins have been consulted for Wheels around Sutton.

to see what vehicles were around at the garage and which vehicles were going in and out". The appeal of some local 'oddball' routes, Peter explained to me "they were nice 'oddball' routes with the S62/63 taking you around much of the Sutton Park perimeter and in the case of the 115/117 the appeal was purely that it was just a peak-hour service [Joint with Walsall Corporation] and to a teenage schoolboy it felt quite an honour to travel on it".

The future of the Midland Red is 'bright' and 'strong'

The first issue of the Clearway in May 1973 was a back on back A4 sheet. Ken Coleclough, District Officer of T & GWU was pleased to see the publication of the mini-bulletin. John Prendergast, holding a similar position in Nalgo, welcomed the mini publication, in addition to the N.B.C. Bus newspaper. General Manager, Mr. Brook, told the MR staff, "I believe the future of Midland Red is bright, offering as it does exciting new developments and the opportunity to emulate the achievements of the past". A two year fleet replacement programme costing more than £2½m is currently being undertaken by the Company. 178 vehicles were expected in 1973, with another 90 in 1974. Mr. S. Lamb, Chief Engineer, said "58 Leyland National vehicles were being delivered early this year with a further 50 ordered to follow by the end of the year". Of the 37 received at that time, Sutton was one of the 7 garages that had "these single door vehicles, 52 seater, powered by a Leyland turbo charged engine capable of developing 200 b.h.p. at 2200 rpm". Sutton Coldfield, along with Birmingham [Adderley Street and Sheepcote Street], Brierley Hill, Dudley, Oldbury and Stourbridge, were the 7 MR properties to be sold to the WMPTE in a £3,600,000 package, stated in Clearway issue 2 of 29th June, 1973. 413 vehicles were to be sold and 1300-1400 staff were involved. All the properties and vehicles fell within the new West Midlands Metropolitan County area. Although 25% of the company's operations were involved in the transfer, Director Robert Brook, saw the MR having a strong future. In the press release it stated "The Midland Red will continue to operate outside the new Metropolitan County area. Indeed, there are several areas of major growth potential for bus services - the two new towns of Redditch and Telford, the towns feeding Coventry and also the greater Leicester area in which the company is the major operator".

"This agreement in no way threatens the existence of Midland Red, rather it presents a new challenge. In the knowledge that it was coming, we have, for many months, been planning how to meet and capitalise on that challenge", said Mr. Brook. Amongst three appointments given was that of Roger Harman's promotion to Assistant Engineer [Operations]. Roger had MR work experience at Banbury, Sutton and Digbeth. There was no Union Column in the June Clearway. The 23rd August, 1973 Clearway rectified that with the reverse side given to the two union reps. Mr. Coleclough considered the sale had been forced on the Midland Red, with Mr. Prendergast not unsimilarly concerned about staff terms and conditions. Mr. Prendergast complimented the Midland Red management on the speed that the General Management explained the situation to representatives from all the workplaces. The NALGO rep reminded MR staff that the 1971 "Operation Phoenix"

Chapter Ten

Sutton's own coach company

The earlier focus of Wheels around Sutton was on the development of stage carriage services by horse, then later using motor driven vehicles for passengers and removals.

My initial premise having lived in Sutton Coldfield from 1935-1963 was that the two pioneer passenger carrying organisations in the Royal Town of Sutton Coldfield were the Midland Red and A.T. Hastilow & Son, the owners of Tudor Rose Coaches. It has been unravelled that neither the BMMO nor Tudor Rose were the first charabanc or coach operators in Sutton, though other firms with the notable exception of Allports did not remain on the public transport scene in that part of Warwickshire and later North Birmingham for long. Eventually the Midland Red from 1913 and A.T. Hastilow from 1921 became the two market leaders in Sutton Coldfield. However, Tudor Rose remained the only long term based coach company based in Sutton, although in 1934 the Midland Red had some coaches operating with its bus fleet from the Upper Holland Road Garage instead of the 21 year import of vehicles and staff from Birmingham premises. I had also wrongly believed that the Park Road removal business of A.T. Hastilow had the distinction of pioneering that type of work in the town. Research has shown that Allports and others offered removal facilities well

before A.T. Hastilow & Son though again, once started, Hastilows became the long term local choice for many Suttonians. A June 1920 advert in the Sutton Coldfield News spoke of 'The Pioneer' chara-banc [in the singular] left Tovey's, at Erdington Village Green for Dovedale, calling at Sutton Coldfield and Four Oaks by appointment. The Hastilow family have been very cooperative in trying to fill in gaps about the firm's early history. They believe the removal business could have begun from 1919, and as earlier noted, the advertising suggested the removal staff had 21 years experience in the business in 1921. The original trading name was A.T. Hastilow & Son, with Alfred Thomas Hastilow the founder. He was father of Alfred Edward Hastilow, who shared in the partnership. The H & S business card shows the son Alfred Edward in NX 5779 and his father Alfred Thomas Hastilow, standing between the two charabancs. Fred Rowan was the driver in the middle coach. Alfred Thomas was a butcher by trade, managing Eastmans the Butchers. We earlier remarked about him being granted a Hackney Carriage licence in Sutton Coldfield during the national rail strike in November 1919. The removal business could have evolved, though it is not certain, from the carting of ice from Birmingham at regular intervals. The family

Broad's Travel strongly promoted Hastilows Tudor Rose Services. Mr Ray Broad leads a toast, with his wife and three sons in the front row for a successful business. (Broads Travel collection)

Driver Harry Watts and the founder Alfred Thomas Hastilow with FWD317, believed to be at a seaside resort, probably Weston Super Mare. (Doug Armstrong collection)

advised me that "additional carriage" was done by Alfred Thomas for other traders. Bob Hemming spoke of "ice being conveyed from Digbeth to Aston, Chester Road and Trows on Sutton Parade". It is known by the family that the senior partner never learned to "drive, whereas son Fred drove when quite young". Prior to being a partner with his dad, "he worked for some time at Moss Gear CO. The following is part of the Hastilow family tree, though a more comprehensive history is available from another member of the extended Hastilow family.

A.T. Hastilow and his immediate family tree

Alfred Thomas Hastilow Elizabeth Hastilow [nee Ford]
Alfred Edward Hilda Hastilow [nee Lawrence]
[known as Fred]
Celia Edward Elizabeth David Susan Mrs. Hilda Hastilow, wife of the founder's only child, Alfred Edward, and the second eldest of Alfred and Hilda's five children, Edward, are the two main family members who have provided me with an insight into the family's view of the business. The Company founder, Mr. A.T. Hastilow died in the 1950s and his heir, Alfred Edward Hastilow, died at the age of 90. An insight into driving instruction and techniques in the 1920s was shared by the Hastilow family. A Mrs. Evans had acquired a car, She had never learned to drive, so at her request, Fred Hastilow "took her out for a drive". She must have been a quick and competent learner, and Mr. Hastilow a good instructor because "she drove the car next day on her own from Sutton into Birmingham to shop at Lewis's. Mrs. Evans left the car outside the store, there was little car traffic then!"

A.T. Hastilow & Son staff

The Hastilows understand that the Park Road development was a "greenfield site, next to back to back houses which extended from the Parade. The opposite corner house belonged to Mr. Fawdry. Fawdry Close is named after him. The coach work began at the formation of the Company. Tudor Rose was the original name". The coach "staff wore white coats with red collars and cuffs and white caps. The coats etc. were washed, starched and ironed very frequently". Some of the maintenance at Park Road Garage meant the "coaches were often repainted ... These were brush painted with eight coats of paint". The people who were employed "before WWII by Hastilows included Syd Burton, Albert Cooper, Fred Rowan and Harry Watts. There was often a cross over of drivers but mainly one way, Coach driver to Removals, as the coach drivers needed the P.S.V. licence". To fit in with the requirements of the weekly service licence the list of destinations and services offered times and dates etc., "had to be published and advertised before the season started to Rhyl, Colwyn Bay and Llandudno". The trips could be seen advertised in "chalk outside the Park Road office. Local companies A.T. Hastilow used were amongst others, printing by Westwood Press at the Driffold, Travel Agents, Broads Travel in Wylde Green, their Accountants were Potter, McGregor, in Mill Street, and their tyres came from Park Road neighbours, Stella Tyres". At the outbreak of WWII, Hastilows had 3 furniture vans and the family think, 4 coaches, 2 of which were taken for war service, but were not returned. It may be the 2 commissioned coaches saw service in France, though it is unconfirmed. Driver Syd Burton showed an enterprising spirit during the war. Having learned that there was work for a "furniture van in abundance on the South Coast of England, he wanted to take a van down there, but this was never done". With the help of Alan Mills, again of the Omnibus Society, a fleet list of A.T. and A.E. Hastilow, Tudor Rose Coaches, of 8, The Parade, Sutton Coldfield, is given until just after WWII. According to the family, the fleet numbers were allocated as the vehicle joined the company, whether it was a coach or a removal van. Although the coaches went to Harper Bros in June 1960, the fleet numbering continued up to number 31 in 1966/7, with only removal vehicles in the last 7 years.

The Omnibus Society list of Tudor Rose Coaches

A.T. & A.E. Hastilow

8 The Parade, Sutton Coldfield, 1921-1947
AC 9984 Daimler CK 26 seater chara April 1921. Rebodied later as C30 EN 1746 Dennis ? seater chara New Jan 1922.

Ex-Davidson, Barry later became lorry/furniture van of Hastilow?

Scrapped March 1931 NX 5779 LVL 14 seater April 1924.

Scrapped March 1932 UE 8214 Dennis 26 seater coach

March 1929 To van UE 8848 Chevrolet 14 seater coach June 1929 sold?

WD 5223 Dennis Lancet ?seater coach March 1933 Rebodied by Yates, Loughborough as C31F Sept 1948.

Fitted with AEC Diesel engine WD 6936 Bedford 20 seater coach. March 1934. sold?

WD 9522 Dennis Lancet Burlingham 32 seat coach

April 1935 commandeered 1940 AUE 265 Dennis Lancet

Dennis 32 seat coach April 1936 commandeered 1940

DWD 885 Bedford Utility 32 seat bus Feb 1943 On wartime permit. Rebodied Duple 29 seats 1948

Little known LVL

One of the early acquired Hastilow vehicles for carrying passengers was by LVL, a company that hardly anyone seemed to have heard of. My interest in the 14 seater, NX 5779, was aroused by the initials LVL on the radiator, seen in the photo shown to me by Mrs Vi Watts of two Tudor Rose charabancs in Station Street, Sutton Coldfield. Alan Mills was one of the folk who responded to my request for help over details about LVL, confirming it was a 14 seater, Hastilows had it "from new in April 1924, and it remained in service until the end of the 1931 service". Black Country Vehicles Historian Jim Boulton also came to my rescue, "on this very little known make, in fact until about 18 months ago [January 1993], when I wrote the book Powered Vehicles made in the Black Country I knew nothing of it at all". Jim had found that Edward Genna launches the "Light Vehicles Limited, firm in late 1923 and it continued to 1926 when the company was liquidated", still operating from Powlett Street, Wolverhampton. NX 5779 was the sixth vehicle built by LVL, its chassis number was A.76, it was a B.14 type, with engine number 16243. The company according to the March 29th, 1924 issue of Motor Commerce, specialised in 25-30 CWT industrial and passenger-coach chassis. The list price at the time was £395, with front wings, step boards and a set of tools. The magazine reported on page 424, "For passenger purposes the chassis carries with little overhang a 14-16 seater coach body. Alternatively it can be supplied as a double-purpose chassis [i.e. for goods and passengers] with a comfortable upholstered three-persons seat and hood and a vertically divided front screen". By the way, Jim Boulton's book was published by the Black Country Society 1976, with the second enlarged edition in 1990. Grandson Edward Hastilow looking with me at the 1921 garage plans pointed out that the small booking office in Park Road, known to thousands of folk over the years, was added on. In competition with the BMMO, Sutton News advert in September 1934 that the large group offered saloon coaches for hire from Sutton garage, A.T. Hastilow ran a 10/- racing return special to Doncaster for the Saint Leger. A week later, the removal side advertised full responsibility accepted up to £1,000 implying other removal companies did not have such comprehensive back-up insurance. Mrs. Burnett remembered an A.T. Hastilow & Son, advertisement in Saxtons Monthly

The big blizzard on Oxford Road, chipping Norton, Oxfordshire on March 29th, 1952. (Frank Facker/Doug Armstrong collection)

Three of Hastilow & Son "Tudor Rose" coaches almost blocking Park Road, adjacent to the Garage. From Left to Right the coaches are WD 5223, A Dennis "Lancet" with full front "Tudor Rose" radiator modernised in Hastilow's workshop, FWD 317, A Dennis "Lancet" with body by W.S. Yeates of Loughborough (A combination much favoured by Hastilows) and FUE 992 a Bedford OB coach with standard 29 seat Duple "Vista" coachwork driver. Harry Watts stands by FWD 317. (Doug Armstrong Collection)

Recorder of January, 1935. Prospective clients were informed "The Tudor Rose Safety Coaches" were "20,26 and 32 seaters". The company asked that they could be allowed to "quote for your outings. Special rates for mid-week parties". A contemporary advert by Rickards of Station Road, Erdington, offered a display of radios from £5.5.0, or 2/5 weekly. The weekly radio hire charge brought back memories of the barrack room radio hire we contributed to

in 1953, at a Royal Engineer unit in Kent. Knowing of my interest in Midland Red operations, Mrs. Burnett included further pages from January 1935 of the large company's services in the Sutton, Erdington areas. The 102/3 timetable gave additional "Picture House Buses from the Wylde Green pavilion, and for Empress patrons at Sutton Parade". Industrial services linking the Royal Town employees with Fort Dunlop departures are shown at 7.30 a.m. for those

The site of the A. T. Hastilow garage was close to the first of the two West Midlands Travel Double Deckers. (Alan Kirkman)

Harry Watts son Tony sitting on a Marshall's coach at Gretna Green in 1949. (Rigby/Doug Armstrong Collection)

coming off the night shift, then two at lunchtime. Saxton's prepaid advertisements informed of Higgs, 280 Gravelly Lane, carried out large or small removals at "strictest economical charges".

Tudor Rose coach sunk in WWII

Amongst the regular and respected Hastilow drivers was Mr. Burton. Syd Burton's widow told me "The drivers had no set hours and no overtime was paid". She recalled he earned £2.15d per week at one stage of his Hastilow career. Staff names that came to mind were : "Fred Rowan, Harry Watts, Arthur Loweth, Bernard Hemming, Albert Cooper, Jimmy Lowndes and Sam Blackwell". Ethel remembered the Government commandeered Tudor Rose Coaches "and the one Syd drove went down at Dunkirk". She added "Hastilow staff went anywhere they were wanted. 2 drivers would go, and accommodation paid for if necessary when spending one or two nights away", on removal work. Another Hastilow staff widow, Mrs. Vi Watt said her late husband Harry, worked for the coach, removal company from 1921-1955. According to Mrs. Watts, Mr. Hastilow told his coach drivers "to take your wives and family if there were vacancies". Vi said "Harry, one Sunday morning, asked her to get ready quickly for a trip to Evesham. When we were in Evesham, Harry asked if she had brought the lunch. As he had not told me to, I hadn't. So he took me to a cafe for lunch!" Over the years Vi accompanied her husband in 'vacant seats' to Dovedale, Symonds Yat, Hampton Court, Windsor, Blehheim Palace and Weston-Super-Mare. A reflection of the odd hours he had to work as a coach driver was accepted by Mrs. Watts. "Harry suffered from the drivers' complaint - tummy trouble. Because of the odd hours he worked, he took his meal times when he could".

Mrs. Burton speaking of Syd, said "he sometimes had lunch with a party according to how far they had travelled. He did not take a packed lunch with him.

Hastilows Parade Dining Rooms

Bob Hemming was born in Station Street, close to A.T. Hastilow's Parade and Park Road premises. Whilst working for the firm from 1928, he enjoyed the faggots, peas and tripe, and cow heels served up at the Parade dining rooms of Hastilows. "The Hastilow staff", I was told by Mr. Hemming, "did not have the meals at reduced prices, but they made lovely faggots and peas". It was while Norman Beech worked as a hairdresser for Walter Bowers, at 34 High Street, opposite the Three Tuns, that he used the cafe. He informed me, "The cafe was run by Miss Hastilow. Tickets for the coach activities were sold there and at the garage. I went for a cooked lunch, Tuesday, Wednesday and Friday. Meat, veg and a sweet in 1937 cost 1/-, it was used by shopkeepers and their assistants". Mr. Beech remembered that a "Gents haircut in 1934 cost 6d, and 5/- in 1964". Miss Olive Colley's earliest memories of A.T. Hastilow include "private party outings arranged by my late mother. It was always comfortable and enjoyable. The driver was always Harry Watts". The Hastilow family thought the most popular service they offered "was the coach to Villa Park, which was parked in the Dog car park and customers paid the driver when boarding". It is that kind of memory that remains with football supporters for many years and retold to children and grandchildren over the decades.

Special rolling mills installed in Park Road

There is something of a mystery over WD 5223 the Dennis

Lancet which joined Tudor Rose in March 1933. The records seem to suggest Hastilows retained the vehicle during WWII and it was rebodied by Yeates of Loughborough in the autumn of 1948, when it was fitted with a AEC diesel engine. Showing Mr. Edward Hastilow a picture of WD 5223 by the late Don Morris, which Mr. T.W. Moore thought may "have been taken at the Villa Park Coach Park", Ted recounted a story about the coach. Similar to what was written concerning the Midland Red's difficulty of obtaining or building new vehicles, "Immediately after WWII coaches could not be had. A new coach body was built onto the old chassis of WD 5223 at Park Road mainly by mechanic Jack Cockayne and my father, 'Fred' Hastilow. To carry out this essential work, special rolling machines were installed to shape the panels". Ted can recall, "walking through the garage I saw the words Tudor Rose in ply, and later it had been cut out in aluminium", to be fixed on the front of the coach.

A.T. Hastilow Tudor Rose coach list completed

Returning to The Omnibus Society list of the eighteen passenger carrying vehicles registered with A.T. & A.E. Hastilow, the remaining post WWII coaches were, in addition to wartime permit vehicle DWD 885 and WD 5223 :

FUE 992 Bedford OB Duple 29 seater coach, April 1947. Sold 1950

FWD 317 Dennis Lancet Yeates 35 seat coach, May 1947. To Harpers, June 1960

GUE 207 Bedford OB Duple 29 seat coach, Feb 1948. Sold 1951

HWD 227 Dennis Lancet Burlingham 33 seat coach, May 1949. Sold Sept 1956

JUE 655 Dennis Lancet Yeates 35 seat coach, Feb 1950. To Harpers June 1960

KUE 373 Dennis Lancet Yeates 39 seat coach, Feb 1951. To Harpers June 1960

NAC 908 Dennis Lancet Yeates 37 seat coach, May 1953. To Harpers June 1960

TWD 672 Commer Avenger Duple 41 seat coach, April 1946. To Harpers June 1960

Mrs. Sally Crockett who, with her husband, ran the grocery shop at the junction of Jerome Road and Ebrook Road in Sutton, went on a Tudor Rose coach with the Kings Arms Darts Team. " I think it was an outing to New Brighton, organised by Mrs. Blower". In the post WWII period, eventually a comprehensive pattern of services were offered from Park Road and other pick up points which included excursions, charter, contract and school work. "Work", the family told me "was done for most schools, the police and GPO". When pressed, additional vehicles "were hired from Tindalls of Tamworth; Dunn Hale, Brownhills; Jackson Coaches, Castle Bromwich; and Sandwell Motor Co., Handsworth". The only time I personally recall a coach breaking down on a Tudor Rose service was on an excursion, I think to Weston-Super-Mare when the hired Blundells vehicle, which was far below the expected high Tudor Rose standards for its own coaches, failed en route.

1957 examples of Tudor Rose Excursions and Tours

Looking back from the last years of the twentieth century, similar to some other contributors, writing about events of forty plus years before, the memories of using Hastilow services may not be in chronological order, but they

A Midland Vehicle at Lichfield Bus station in 1996. (Mike Concannon)

Harry Watts with a party of 20 ladies he had conveyed to Southport, believed to be before WWII. (Doug Armstrong Collection)

happened! Because of that one failure of a Hastilow service, it stands out against the many pleasurable times with my parents, Albert, Polly, and younger brother David, when we

A 1955 Broad's booklet of inclusive Coach holidays they promoted with a number of company's including Hastilows. (Broads Travel Collection)

travelled with Tudor Rose coaches. As I grew up, I had the enjoyment of going to the company's small booking office, adjoining the garage in Park Road, to book the excursions my parents had selected, checking the chalk written alternatives on the board outside. The initial information about the programme offered, was often seen in the weekly Sutton Coldfield News, or the monthly 'Tudor Rose' Coach Tours leaflet, printed by W.S. Iliffe and Son at 89-90 Bradford Street, Birmingham 12. Using Cliff Griffin's example of 1957, not long before the Harper take over, the longest Sunday trips, both for 20/-, were Southsea and Bournemouth. Both tours were timed to pick up at 14 locations. Starting at 6.45 a.m. from the Hardwick Arms, the points included 7 am, Little Sutton [Fox and Dogs]; 7.10, Hastilow's Garage; 7.25, the Fox at Walmley and finally Broad's [Erdington Bus Terminus] at 7.30 am. The midweek fares to the same destinations came down to 16/9, rising to 22/3 for Bournemouth on a Bank Holiday Tuesday. A further variety of seaside venues that could be visited midweek for 14/- each were : Burnham-on-Sea, Clevedon, Weston-Super-Mare, Barry Island, Aberdovey, Aberystwyth, Barmouth, Colwyn Bay, New Brighton via the Mersey Tunnel, Southport and Skegness. Favourite stately homes and popular buildings from the Sutton area were : Blenheim Palace, Woburn Abbey, Haddon Hall, Windsor, and Chatsworth House. Other inland locations offered at intervals were : Hereford, Tenbury, Leominster, Wickstead park, Bourton-on-the-Water., Bakewell, Matlock, Warwick and Stratford, The Peak District and Castleton, Cotswolds, Ludlow, Pershore and Evesham, Tewkesbury, Broadway, Symonds Yat, Malvern and Upton. Amongst a number of annual flower shows, Hastilows arranged to go to Southport and Shrewsbury, whilst evening tours could include a mystery destination, or a visit to Leamington Lights. An evening tour my father took me on was to the Stratford Mop.

A selection of Tudor Rose outings shown outside Broad's Travel Bureau and General Hardware shop at Chester Rd Tram Terminus. (Broad's Travel Collection)

I was fascinated by the variety of colourful stalls, the tempting aromas from the locations selling different types of cooked food, the excitement around the amusement rides, and the historic buildings of Shakespeare's town. It was a stunning, unexpected experience for a young person from a council estate, with limited opportunities to expand his knowledge of the UK's vast heritage. Thanks to Hastilows, I gained a little more insight. With a small homely company like A.T. Hastilow & Son, it was inevitable the regular customers or patrons soon knew the drivers, with a bond of trust and friendship building up which was not always possible with Midland Red passengers because their day to day services had different objectives and a much larger work force. With the Tudor Rose school, club and works contracts, the school children, social club members or factory workers had a few limited permutations of who was to drive their vehicle to school, outing venue or factory gate! The town, village or roadside cafe where the driver stopped for the morning coffee and toilet break was part of the excursion day trip, with names such as Tewkesbury, Melton Mowbray and Knutsford coming to mind before the M5, M42 and M6. In the company of what seemed the majority of coach firms, the Tudor Rose drivers left the day out seaside resorts around 5 pm. it seemed to be a hallowed hour, to get back to the Sutton Coldfield pick up points by 10.15 pm. The maximum time at the customers' chosen resort was around 5 hours but could be 4 hours depending on distance and traffic congestion. How long the visitors spent on the sands and in the sea could also be reduced in trying to find a

clean, reasonably priced cafe selling fish and chips, if a packed lunch was not taken. There was usually a toilet stop on the return journey, combined with the availability of at least one nearby pub. On some occasions if there had been delays in reaching the venue, less time was given for the evening stop, or on occasions left out, much to the annoyance of the pub regulars. David Hastilow who drove for Hastilows from 1953-1956 has a drinker's story that made me feel sick.

Reputation of Sutton Coldfield tarnished in the Cotswolds

David told me "A party of 2 Sutton Councillors with local Council staff including 3 women, it was almost a full coach, went from a Mere Green pub to the Cotswolds on a very hot summer day. I got to Mere Green for 7.45 am. The boot was loaded up with crates of beer. There were so many crates, I could not get any more in the boot, so the overflow was stored in the coach. We left at 8 am. The party members immediately started to drink the beer. We had got the other side of Stonebridge when there was a request for some to get out because they had been caught short. They went some distance from the coach. The drinking continued on their return and the stops became more frequent". The party members were in such a state according to David they only managed to get out of the vehicle before they "peed up the side of the coach". During the Stow-on-the-Wold lunch stop "one of the men put his hand up a waitress's skirt". The

Harry Watts on right, with colleague in front of FWD 317. (Doug Armstrong Collection)

whole party was quickly dismissed from the premises by the restaurant management. The name of Sutton Borough Council was tarnished that day in the Cotswolds. For David, the day was far from over. He asked for further instructions. It was afternoon, should they go on to Bourton- on-the-Water, the party's booked destination? No. They wanted to get back to the Mere Green pub. They had had enough of the Cotswolds. The driver, trying to ensure they had the chance to see the lovely countryside, on such a lovely day

with the sunroof fully opened, took them home via Stratford on Avon, Warwick and Kenilworth. Driver Hastilow was not aware there had been a heavy rain storm in that part of Warwickshire. "In those days" David continued "the road went through a shallow ford at Kenilworth. However, as I approached the ford at 30 mph it was much deeper than usual. With so much water on the road and the speed, the cooling water surged up the coach side, soaking the party members through the open sunroof". The worst was still to

The changed front of WD5223 which Mr. Ted Hastilow saw in the making.

come, according to the Tudor Rose driver. A little later on, the weather changed with a thick fog coming down. Fortunately, David found an articulated Adams Butter vehicle in front of him, and he followed his tail lights. Presumably, the Mere Green bound party were back at their heavy drinking routine because David was told to stop straight away as members were being "caught short". He had to refuse because the visibility was poor and the road was not suitable to stop in. He gave a member of the party the inspection hatch key, with strict instructions which hatch and how to lift it, so they could urinate into the hatch. Carrying along in the fog, there were screams from the passengers. "You must pull up" they demanded. To David's horror, one man with diarrhoea, had opened another hatch, "doing his job through the hole, it hit the differential, went on the universal coupling, it was thrown up the side of the coach and back into the coach via the open sunroof, over the party" including the trouser- down man. The coach eventually got the drunken party to the Mere Green pub to continue their drinking and leave David to clean up a filthy coach. Another group he recalls were a trainspotters club "they were as mad as hatters! Once you started the tour, it was non- stop. They had packed meals and vacuum flasks, the driver had to take the same with him, eating as he drove". The routine was "take the engine number, then catch it up to photograph it. At least they knew exactly where they wanted to go, having detailed maps to guide you with. At the time we earned 2/6 an hour. Those trainspotters were very good to the driver, though it was a long, hard day, because they were very liberal with their money as the hat went round the coach!"

Weston - local resort choice

In the winter months David assisted with the removal, transport side of the business. "When I was there they had 2 vans, a Dennis and a Ford Trader. We often went to Beatties in Birmingham to collect furniture and deliver it. I would not like the removal work on a regular basis". Speaking of his relationship with A.T. Hastilow and Son, David informed me, "The old fellow was a cousin to my grandfather. I am not sure what that makes me!" When the drivers arrived back in the evening, the founder bought them a drink at the Museum, his son was there as well. In about 1955/6 "the old fellow did not come down so much and Arthur Loweth was made the Office Manager". David remembers the autumn illumination specials. "In October we went to Blackpool. We left Sutton at 10.30 am on the Saturday morning, returning from Blackpool at 12.30 am next morning, arriving back in Sutton around 5.30 am. You could be out again that morning on another job. We did work 18-20 hour days, with actual driving around 10 hours per day. We could get our rest when the passengers were not on the coach". Weston-Super-Mare appeared to be a favourite for many Suttonians. However, many hundreds a month in the peak holiday periods must have been disappointed or frustrated, or both, to find there was no sea to be seen at Weston, just miles of mud. Even so, the day outings, some were also offered by the railways, were enjoyed by folk around the Sutton district, giving them a change of scenery. John Raines wrote that his recollections from the early 1950s reminded him that "Weston-Super-Mare was a popular destination, the journey taking 5 hours, with a break at Tewkesbury. Arrival at

Several Stockland Burlingham bodied Leylands are shown parked at the rear of Stockland's spacious garage in 1947. Leyland HOM 778 is seen in the centre of the photograph and a Bedford "OB" can be seen on the extreme right. (K. A. F. Brewin)

Weston was at 1.0 pm and departure was at 5.0 pm". Mr. Raines refers to "afternoon trips to Evesham in the summer and I can remember everyone coming back laden with huge baskets of plums. The return itinerary included a stop at Stratford-on-Avon". John preferred the excursions to the Morecambe rather than Blackpool Illuminations, "though it was a less popular destination than Blackpool and the small Bedford coach was often used". He continued "I can remember a very foggy return in this coach on one occasion. As we reached home, most of the passengers were asleep and were rudely awoken by a sudden application of the brakes. We had collided with a wooden barrier guarding a deep excavation in the Chester Road and had stopped right on the brink of it". Rather than disappoint its customer, Hastilows, on occasions combined the passengers going to two destinations, into one vehicle but called at both locations, like Blackpool and Morecambe.

Morecambe via Blackpool

Such was the situation one autumn Saturday. Having called at Blackpool first with "no coast road between the two resorts" John informed me, "one has to go back inland to rejoin the A6 near Garstang, adding an hour to the journey, so we didn't arrive at Morecambe until 2.0 pm. The day was a very wet one and everybody was back in the coach by 11.30 pm, but the driver told us that he was not allowed to leave the coach park before midnight. Those waiting at Blackpool had almost given up hope when they were picked up at 1.0 am!" For some Tudor Rose drivers who were diagrammed to take another day excursion later that day, they cleaned the coach before going home, otherwise the cleaning was done when he returned later in the day, perhaps to take out an afternoon or evening trip. Mrs. Mary Bryan of Cleveland, patronised Hastilow removal and coach departments. Mary's regular "day trips each year with my children" led to a request from Tudor Rose Coaches. "it was

while I was at Falcon Lodge Crescent that Hastilows asked me and another lady to go to court for them to get a licence to run trips to the South Coast, which they got". The company moved Mrs. Bryan to Cambridgeshire in 1961. The Hastilow family advised me that on occasions after WWII when they were very busy on the removal side, Bakers of Erdington and Lewis's deliveries were called in to assist. Ray Jennings was a Hastilows coach and removal van driver from 1953-55, the rate of pay was "about 2/6 per hour. I did removal work when coach work was slack. Most weekends we did service work to Rhyl, Colwyn Bay and Llandudno. The fares being about 10/-, 12/-, and 14/-. If we were required to do private work then, the services were contracted out". I asked Ray about his impressions of the Tudor Rose fleet. The company allocated Ray to Harry Watts vehicle KUE 373, when the respected long term driver left. Mr. Jennings said "KUE was a Dennis six cylinder diesel with a Yeates Body from Loughborough. It was a robust coach, 8' across the front wings and 7'6" at the back. As the largest vehicle in the fleet, you had to watch the width in parts of Wales". Ray went on, "The 39 seater had a top speed of approx 65 mph with an unladen weight of 6 tons 16 cwt. The brakes were fair, but not great. The boot of the coach was very close to the road and used to scrape quite often making a row". During his time with Hastilows he associated the following drivers with individual Tudor Rose coaches: FWD 317 Fred Stretch HWD 227 Dave Hastilow and NAC 908 Frank Andrews. According to Ray all the drivers helped each other with a good working spirit amongst all the Hastilow staff. He thought the most popular places were those in North Wales. One stopping place that came to him was Praise Heath, in Shropshire. He thought there had to be a minimum of 15 adult fare paying passengers to make an excursion viable, though driver David Hastilow gives a lower figure. Mr. Jennings eventually drove for Hastilows, Harper Brothers and the Midland Red. I asked him if he preferred one more than the other two. He told me "Hastilows was the

Stockland Garage in Marsh Hill, Erdington (the Birmingham district adjoining Sutton, Coldfield) became a major operator in postwar years, pioneering cross-channel tours to France, Belgium, Switzerland, Germany and Holland. The fleet consisted mainly of new heavy-weight Leyland half cab coaches bodied by H. V. Burlingham of Blackpool and Santus Motor Bodies of Wigan with 33 seater luxury bodies. For lighter duties, Stockland also operated a number of Bedford OB coaches with Duple "Vista" 29 seat bodies. HOB 941, newly delivered and a good example of Stockland's two tone blue "OB's", is shown in 1947 in lonely isolation in front of Stockland's impressive garage which was crowned with a clock tower and also contained a booking office. Stockland had a number of local pickup points but used such agents as Scattergoods of Washwood Heath rather than Broad's in Erdington.
(K. A. F. Brewin)

best, with a fair boss and decent vehicles". Ray remembered the founder owner of Hastilows, "wore a hard hat and winged collar, visiting the Museum pub for a drink".

"Don't phone the boss!"

Driver David Hastilow queried with Mr. Hastilow Senior, that the 39 seater coach allocated next day in the 1950s to Weston- Super-Mare had only 6 customers. Mr. Hastilow told David, "They have paid their money, they will go". David advised me that "round trip with just 6 cost more than a month's wages paid to me". David received a shock at the Weston Coach Park. "I was besieged by holidaymakers, mainly from the Chester Road area who could not get back from holiday because of the rail strike. I returned with a total of 56. The boot and racks were filled with luggage, and the cases down the aisles had children sitting on them!" Apparently the unbooked passengers were very appreciative of his kindness but David said to them, "Don't phone the boss on Monday and thank him or I will get the sack". Alan Washbrook of Haxby, Yorkshire, recalled Bishop Vesey Grammar School used Hastilows coaches, and he went on them as a pupil. He was impressed with the service given. Mr. D. Townsend still recalls travelling on Tudor Rose Coaches "on Coronation Day with the rest of the local children to Sutton Park where a tea party was held at the old Crystal Palace". One evening, David Hastilow was returning to the garage after dropping off his last passengers, when he was stopped by excited Hastilow driver colleagues near the

Museum public house. Like David they were members of a pools syndicate, contributing 2/6 a week. Checking the numbers they realised their selection had hit the £45,000 jackpot that week in the 1950s. A real fortune. David was delighted to hear the news but suggested they postpone their celebrations until they saw the money. One driver however, started buying drinks to celebrate, at the Museum. David continued to the garage, washing his coach for the next day's assignment. David informed me "the money had been paid out, but none of the syndicate members received any. It was rumoured the syndicate secretary went to live in Australia!"

Broad Travel Innovations

Broads Travel Bureau was synonymous with coach travel in the North Birmingham and Sutton Coldfield area to me as a young person in the late 1940s, early 1950s, though it provided a wider travel service, than just coach transport. Founder Mr. Ray Broad described the development of his successful travel organisation in a 3 page feature in the March 1974 Coaching Journal, under the title of 'Forty years plus in travel', tracing the start in early 1931, from his father's established hardware business, close to the Erdington Tram Terminus. Ray Broad showed his commitment to his customers by opening his office after WWII, at the height of the season "at 2 am for the 2.33 am coach to Ealing, and on many weeks remained open until the 4.15 am to Liverpool". I was interested to learn from the family that the founder

An excited group of North Birmingham holiday-makers about to leave with Hastilows for a week's holiday in Llandudno. C.1948. At the front is a Dennis Lancet with WS. Yeates body in the centre is a Bedford Dupte OB whilst a Leyland brings up the rear. (Broads Travel Collection)

with PSV licence number DD 18050, drove for Mr. Hastilow at regular intervals not long after WWII. Ray Broad was also known to drive for Tindalls. The 1956 Broads inclusive holidays brochure listed 8 day tours to : The Isle of Man; Blackpool; Morecambe; English Lakes and Scottish Borders; The Scottish Lochs; Scotland centred at Dunoon; Northern Ireland and Llandudno and North Wales. The latter one was operated by Tudor Rose Coaches. The holiday centred at the Grafton Private Hotel costing £12.0.0d in May-June, September, and £12.12s in the high season. The holiday included a visit to the Isle of Anglesey, Menai Straits and Swallow Falls. The route from Birmingham in 1953 was via Whitchurch, Mold, and St. Asaph arriving at Llandudno at 3.0 pm in $6\frac{1}{4}$ hours. The return service, with an apparent $\frac{1}{2}$ hour break, left at 3.30 pm from the Royal Red Coach Station, with a short stop at Whitchurch, arriving in Birmingham around 9.0 pm. Incidentally, Saxtons Monthly Recorder of June 1939, prices a similar 8 days holiday to Llandudno and North Wales, from Broads Travel Bureau by the Tram Terminus at £5.17.6d.

Hastilow ledger secrets

A further perspective of Hastilow coach, general transport and removal work from just before WWII until the company's Tudor Rose sale to Harper Bros, was kindly made

available by the Hastilow family loaning me a ledger recording Broad Travel Bureau transactions on behalf of the Park Road firm, as well as the Sutton Centre's own record of work. The ledger entries back up many recollections by people already noted. In 1938, the Sutton Borough Treasure's Department hired Hastilows to carry out a removal to Ebrook Road in April for £1.10.0d, followed by moving furniture to the Holland Estate, for £3.15.0d, and a similar venture to Withy Hill Road, at £1.2.6d, all in May of the same year. Another body with authority, Sutton Police, used a Tudor Rose vehicle to travel to Warwick in February, 1938, PC Roberts apparently was involved with the arrangements. The Police used Hastilow coaches on 29 occasions that year, whilst again in 1938, Wylde Green College scholars were transported to Lichfield for £1.1.0d; Stourbridge, Coleshill, Acocks Green; and to Dudley Zoo, costing £8.0.0d in July. With the groving threat of a second world war in 1939, the Police made 16 hirings up to August, some of coaches, others were vans to convey furniture, whilst the Treasurer's department had Nurse Barker's effects removed for £2.0.6d on the 29th September that year. War or no war, Bishop Vesey Grammar School took coach parties in 1940 to Warwick and Atherstone, probably for cricket or athletic events and to Walsall in the autumn for a likely rugby fixture. There was an outing to Whittington, perhaps Army Cadet Force related on the 7th February, 1941, for

£2.0.0d, whereas the Sutton Police paid for 7 furniture removals between 1940-44, visiting Queen Street, Tudor Road and Springfield Road. In November, 1944, BVGS had an Army Cadet Force coach trip to an unnamed destination! Princess Alice's Orphanage had a piano taken to Handsworth in June 1942, and 4 months later had goods moved to Sutton Town Hall and back to P.A.O. Early in the spring of 1945, coach journeys were made to Coventry and Wolverhampton by Orphanage children and staff. The bad debts account saw a farmer in Wales owing £6.15.0d in June, 1944, and a Local Home Guard Unit £2.0.0d, a year later a coach company was £5.0.0d in arrears. It was election time in July 1945, when transport was provided for the Surveyor's Department to convey ballot boxes over 4 days.

Hastilow excursions begin again in July 1945

Though money was scarce for some in 1945, and the local garage staff of the BMMO were on strike on Sunday 15th July, the Broads Travel Bureau account shows Tudor Rose Coaches operated public tours that day to Evesham, Milford and Hoars Cross. In August, folk around Erdington and Sutton Coldfield were taken by A.T. Hastilow and Son to some old seaside favourites, barred to many in the war years, such as New Brighton, Weston, Rhyl and Llandudno. The Broads records show further half day and day

A listing of one month's Tudor Rose Coach Tours in 1957. (Cliff Griffin)

excursions were provided on Tudor Rose vehicles in September 1945. It would seem the local small company, probably with an easier staffing situation, and no strike threats, quickly adapted to the requests of the excursion starved local community to get out and see their coastline and country areas after the war. The BMMO management quickly recognised their public's demand for excursions and extended tours, but regrettably they could not respond as quickly as the Park Road team. The MR priority was the provision of daily stage carriage services. The enthusiasm and support from agents like Broads must have attracted customers in the Chester Road, Erdington districts, to use the outings offered by Hastilows, and other coach operators.

1945 Christmas post

In November 1945, the Sutton Girls High School took a party by coach to Smethwick for £2.10.0d and to Edgbaston for a similar amount. The Telephone Manager, at Telephone House, Newhall Street, Birmingham, received the accounts for the GPO hire on 26 occasions to assist with the Christmas post, between 14th- 24th December, with a further van hire on the 27th. The Hastilow coach excursions began in April 1946, to Stratford, Evesham and Tewkesbury. A removal to 112 Perry Common Road cost £36.0.0d; transporting for Ansells Brewery of Park Road, Aston, £5.10.0d; 19/- to Dr. Amos, at High Street, Sutton, and Allport of 5 Station Street, Sutton, were charged £14.2.0d for removal work. Chetwyn House School, Streetly Lane, Sutton hired a coach on 4 occasions between October-March 1947 to take scholars to Anstey College, at £1.10.0d a time. In the summer term the Anstey trip alternated each week with Rectory Park. Work was also carried out for the Reverend McQuilly with the Abbey Schools. Anstey College in 1947 had Hastilow

An Hastilow advert in a 1935 publication.

A fascinating photograph taken post world war I, circa 1921, showing two coaches of the Hastilow fleet and an early removal van outside Hastilows Park Road garage post world war I.

coaches to convey their students to Birmingham University and Kingstanding Baths. Mr. Pullen of High Clare School, Wylde Green hired a coach regularly to take scholars in 1947 to lunch, at 15/- per occasion. The ledger records goods during 1947/8 were transported by Hastilow vans, amongst other places to Nuneaton, Northampton, London, Guildford, Newcastle under Lyme and Manchester. Evertaut Ltd of Walsall Road, Perry Barr, contracted the Park Road vans to deliver goods to Leicester and Cardiff. Wright at 14, The Parade, Sutton, used the company to transport and store a machine at £10.10.0d a month. Having given a flavour of the coach, transport and removal work undertaken by A.T. Hastilow and Son in the 10 years immediately before and after the second world war, a number of further examples are taken from the ledger up to 1960.

Orange Grove Ballroom and Twickenham Pilgrimage

The Reverend Dr. Boggan saw Hastilow vans at the Coleshill Road, Sutton Coldfield Rectory when furniture was packed to travel to Ireland. The railway charges to Belfast were £2.4.5d in April, 1948. The entries in the ledger often give the most basic details, leaving a lot to the reader's imagination to work out the purpose of some bookings. For 9 months from October 1948, Mr. Thomas, a Dance Master, appears to have hired a coach/es to make 2/3 journeys a day, 3 days week to bring clients in from Erdington and Kingstanding to the Orange Grove Ballroom, at Pat Collins, Crystal Palace on the edge of Sutton Park. Whether Mr. Thomas gave dancing lessons, led dancing teams, ran afternoon tea dances, the booking information does not disclose! It does suggest however, that Tudor Rose coaches were used for a wide variety of activities by individuals, clubs and organisations in the Sutton and North Birmingham areas, including the continued patronage by schools. From December 1948, Bishop Vesey's Grammar School hired a

Tudor Rose coach, each year until Hastilows ceased operations in 1960, for the annual rugby pilgrimage to Twickenham, with the exception of 1957. The cost being £26.0.0d in the first year and £27.0.0d three years later. A number of the schools mentioned earlier remained faithful to ATH, whilst the company operated from Park Road. Broads Travel Bureau had a rush for pantomime trips in the 1953/54 prechristmas season, with requests for the Alex, Aston Hippodrome, Birmingham Rep and the Theatre Royal. The travel agents continued to bring in considerable revenue from their Erdington/Chester Road contacts. The Hastilow weekly services to Margate and North Wales remained steady favourites, particularly Rhyl, Colwyn Bay and Llandudno. Broads booked passengers on 18 Saturdays in the 1955 season, selling £984.5.9d worth of tickets over 16 Saturdays in 1957. Works contracts remained another source of vital revenue as A.T. Hastilow and Son saw the increasing evidence of car ownership in the late 1950s with the overall decline of patronage for their coach activities. Hams Hall was a regular user at one time, like GEC Witton, Valor Works, Dunlop and Nechells Power Station. Services for coal miners went to Kingsbury and Rugeley. In the last four years of the Hastilow operations from the Park Road garage, work was contracted with Falcon Lodge Coaches, Holbecke Road, Sutton Coldfield; Flights Coaches, Victoria Road, Aston; Jackson Coaches, Castle Bromwich; and the Sandwell Motor Co. Ltd. of Handsworth. So the ledger of coach activities ends in 1960, though the removal entries continue into the 1960s. The examples taken from the ledger show the operations of Hastilows from a number of angles, including the important Broads Travel Bureau import between 1938 and 1960, the last twenty two years of Tudor Rose's Sutton Coldfield based, thirty nine years history. The next perspective of A.T. Hastilow & Son and its buy out by Harper Bros. requires a recap of the Heath Hayes company's development.

Chapter Eleven

Harper's further growth and end

It was the intention of "Wheels around Sutton" to trace the formation and development of the Midland Red and A.T. Hastilow & Son. This brief was later extended to include more material on Harper Brothers because of their eventual buying out of the Park Road firm. However, cooperation from the Harper family was not forthcoming owing to their full diary of events, so the views on Harpers are limited to customers and knowledgeable staff. Harpers, like Hastilows, were well respected in their area. Their former Traffic Manager, from 1946 to the Midland Red's takeover in April, 1974, Mr. E.J. Eccleshall, then as Superintendent at Heath Hayes until it closed on 6th February, 1976, provided some more information about the company. Incidentally, Mr. Eccleshall was then promoted to Divisional Traffic Manager [North West Division] until his retirement in September, 1981. Similar to the BMMO and A.T. Hastilow we need to retrace our steps to WWII to find out how Harpers operated in the war years. Mr. Eccleshall himself was a prisoner of war in Poland rejoining Harpers in the summer of 1945. Mr. Eccleshall informed me "During WWII all Harpers Bros staff remained in reserved occupations and in addition to operating Stage Carriage Services between Cannock and Aldridge - Cannock - Calf Heath - Brewood, operated factory services to G.E.C. and Kynock's, Witton and Ordnance Factory at Featherstone, and Four Ashes factories. I understand that coaches 16 & 17 [Leyland Tiger Diesel] were taken over by the War Department, but I have no first hand information on this".

Harper Bros services

To indicate the development of the Harper Bros services up to the time they were taken over, Mr. Eccleshall gave this list of licences HB operated, included the vital works services from WWII. Stage Carriage To Birmingham from Cannock via Leacroft, Heath Hayes, Norton Canes, Brownhills, Shire Oak, Walsall Wood, Aldridge, Streetly, Kingstanding, Perry Barr, to Carrs Lane, Birmingham. From Cannock via Cross Keys, Heath Hayes an then as above. From Boney Hay, Chase Terrace, Burntwood, Chasetown, Ogley Hay, Shire Oak, Chester Road, Little Aston, Hardwick Arms, Kingstanding, Perry Barr to Carrs Lane. The other service to Carrs Lane ran from Hednesford, Chadsmoor, Cannock, Bridgtown, Cheslyn Hay - M6 to A34 then Perry Barr, Carrs Lane. The Lichfield [Levetts Fields] service to Kingstanding ran vi a Chesterfield, Wall, Shenstone, Stonnall, Shire Oak, Walsall Wood, Aldridge and Streetly, whereas the Aldridge [Circular] operated via Northgate, Leighswood Avenue, Broadmeadow, Lancaster Avenue, Jessie Road, Walton Road, Walsall Wood Road and back into Aldridge

The Cannock to Brewood service called at Hatherton, Four Crosses, Calf Heath and Four Ashes, whilst a similar service only went as far as Calf Heath. Harpers four Works Services went from : the Cannock to Four Ashes factories. A further service ran from Wimblebury via Littleworth , Cross Keys, Heath Hayes,Norton Canes, Brownhills West, Walsall Wood, Aldridge on to G.C.E., Hardy Spicer and I.C.I. at Witton. Covering 3 shifts at Streetly Works was a service from Heath Hayes via Norton Canes, Brownhills, Walsall Wood and Aldridge. The 3 shifts at the Ordnance Factory at Featherstone ran from the Heath Hayes and Cannock area. A further set of significant services operated by Harpers was the Season Express runs. Resorts served were : Torquay, Bournemouth, Southsea, Clacton, Skegness, Blackpool, Prestatyn, Rhyl, Towyn, Colwyn Bay, Llandudno, Betws-y-Coed, Caernarvon, Bangor, Conway, Llandudno Junction, Bala, Dolgelly, Barmouth,, Harlech, Portmadoc, Pwllheli [Butlins], Aberystwyth and Weston- Super-Mare. Harpers ran extended eight-day tours to Devon, Scotland and the Lake District and undertook a considerable amount of private hire work.

Missing rear wheels and wheel nuts

Dorothy Hooper recalled the weekly summer express services and the "Bank Holiday and occasional day trips to the coast, and other areas popular with day trippers, such as Chester, the Cotswolds etc., and occasional Sunday evening mystery tours. Due to the excellent service they provided" she continued "and the reasonable fares, they were very popular with many holiday makers in the Lichfield, Rugeley and Chase areas". Sidney Whittaker speaking of the company's "first Double Decker I believe it was red, rather noisy and about 1940, at a guess". Talking of Gloria-de-Luxe tickets, they were "a thin card type. Brownhills from Brownhills West was 1$\frac{1}{2}$d, 50p in 1994". Sidney spoke of "one driver who was named Sam. He was very popular with passengers, always very friendly, he always stopped at my Grandmother's home to pick her up and drop her off on return. One day a different driver refused to stop for her) my Grandmother complained at Harpers who sided with her against the driver concerned". Mr. Whittaker shared a lovely story that has probably never got into the authoritative Harper Bros records. "One day around 1936" he informed me, "one of Harpers buses [empty] lost its two rear wheels in Wilkin Road, at the time we had a haulage business. We lent the driver a lorry jack to pick up his vehicle while I cycled back to Brownhills looking for wheel nuts and found about 5. Mary Harper was a good friend of my late Grandmother, who used to organise coach trips for Harpers". Sidney considered public opinion of Harper Bros services and staff was "very good indeed, all buses pretty well on time. In the early days people knew most drivers and later on most conductors by first names". Bob Jordan informed me "I was

One of the A T Hastilow & Son, Tudor Rose Coaches sold to Harper Bros in June 1960. The Dennis Lancet 39 seater joined the Park Road fleet in February 1950. JUE 655 in Harper Bros Livery is at Blackpool.

born in Heath Hayes and I remember 'Gloria De Luxe' coaches, that was a name that Harper Bros used when I was a boy. My Dad had a part-time job as Bus Conductor with Harper's buses - he used to work the Brummie speedway specials, he got me smuggled in for nothing under the large heavy drivers overcoat! Mary used to run the office at Heath Hayes, then at High Green, Cannock 'til they got swallowed up by Midland Red". Mr. Whittaker recalled Harper drivers "Joe Martin and Jack Handy and Conductress Edie Morehead".

Keeping in line with 'Ting-Ting'

David Hastilow worked for Harpers for a year in 1956/7 before emigrating to Australia. "The regular Harper drivers drove the coaches, whilst more recent employees worked on the service routes. We had a conductress nicknamed 'Ting-Ting' because she never rang the bell, instead she stamped her foot on the bus floor twice and called out 'ting-ting'. She was my conductor on a Lichfield-Aldridge service leaving at 0650. I told her we would keep to time". She informed me "it can't be done. It's never been done". We left Lichfield on time. We kept straight to the schedule, and were on time at all the stops. 'Ting-Ting' told me as we went down Shire Oak hill "that a large crowd of passengers would be waiting to get on at the stop round the corner. There were 3. I did see some people running down their drives with one arm in the mac, and others running whilst eating toast. We completed the journey on time". David was not

congratulated back at the Heath Hayes garage. The manager at the garage had received complaints about the service running to time! "He was very unhappy with me" conceded David. However, "as David kept strictly to the timetable", nothing else was said. David remained on the service for the remainder of the week. Each morning after the first journey "the passengers were there on time. But the service probably went back to being 15 minutes late every morning". One would anticipate a few of the passengers preferred a bus service that ran to time. I had hoped to learn from the Harper Bros management what reasons led them to decide to purchase Tudor Rose Coaches. With hindsight it appears to have been part of a systematic policy of buying up smaller companies in the West Midlands that had licences, which normally rarely came on to the market. Such licences and businesses, one presumed Harpers required to expand their services further into Staffordshire, and Warwickshire and the West Midlands conurbation. Mr. Eccleshall wrote of other "coach companies which Harper Bros took over in post world war two years included : A.P. Sanders, Chasetown [Silent Night Coaches]; Dunn & Hale [Glider Coaches], Brownhills; and the E and T Licences of J. Heames [purchased from W.M. Hayes Coaches] Walsall". The Tudor Rose collection of licences would certainly have interested the Harper Bros management. Incidentally, Harper Bros was "still a Ltd Company and meetings are held" at one of the Harper homes, according to a letter of September 15th, 1993.

Reason for Hastilow sale

I could not find any reference in the local newspapers to the intended closure of A.T. Hastilow's coach side of the business, or when it ceased in June, 1960. A number of people remembered the cancelling of excursions. This happened to our family a few times, causing much disappointment. Somehow we expected that sufficient other patrons in the Royal Borough would book to enable the trips we were interested in to run on our council estate, the majority of tenants in the 1950s depended on public transport, though a few neighbours in certain business ventures, began to run a van or car and started to use them for leisure. Without us being aware of it at first, Suttonians like so many others in the country began to choose the convenience of a private car over public transport. The Hastilow family noticed in the early fifties the decrease in the take up of their Tudor Rose coach services with a steady decline during the fifties which led them to decide to sell the coach operations. In discussion with the family I wondered if there were a number of considerations they had in mind when they decided whether to put up the Tudor Rose business for sale. They told me the sale decision was "financial only", and they decided not to advertise. Their strategy which appeared to be successful was that "Hastilows wrote to companies whom were thought may be interested in buying" and Harper Bros as a management group buying up smaller coach firms, saw that Tudor Rose activities with its licence and local goodwill of 39 years fitted in well to its overal future policy in the West Midland area. I gained the impression it was not an easy decision for the Hastilow family to sell part of Sutton's main coach company that was born just after WWI, grew in the 1930s, survived WWII and expanded again in the early 1950s before car ownership persuaded people away from public transport. On the plus side for the Hastilow family to sell was the Harper Bros decision to continue offering similar services as Hastilows, within a larger and wider organisation. A further plus important to the Sutton company employers was that the Tudor Rose staff faced "no job losses, with the drivers moved on to removals". No staff went to Harpers. Mrs. Burton advised me of Harpers having "a booking office in Park Road in one of the cottages they bought".

5 Tudor Rose coaches go to Harper Bros

It seems with little media coverage, in June, 1960, Tudor Rose coach operations were sold to Harper Bros, and the full fleet of five moved to Staffordshire. The five were : FWD 317; JUE 655; KUE 373; NAC 908; and TWD 672. The hearing for the take over by Harpers was heard and approved by the Chairman of the West Midlands Traffic Area, which at the time was in York House, Great Charles Street, Birmingham. Mr. Eccleshall attended the court "for the transfer of Excursion and Tour licences together with a limited number of works and schools licences. There was also period express services to Margate, Rhyl, Colwyn Bay and Llandudno, which were operated until the take over by Midland Red". Harper's Traffic Manager emphasised the company "developed almost daily excursions from Sutton Coldfield [Parade] and area which included Streetly, Blake Street, Four Oaks, Walmley, Mere Green, Reddicap Heath, Yenton, New Oscott, Wylde Green, Erdington and Whitehouse Common". People were beginning to notice the new acquisition by Harpers. Roger de Boer wrote to say "it was the summer of 1960 that I went with my mother to Colwyn Bay catching JUE 655 at Erdington - the Harper Brothers pick up point for that trip. On the return journey I was disappointed at first because we were allocated to NAC 908 which had travelled in convoy with JUE. Now this was

Former Tudor Rose, JUE 655 as Harper Bros, No.54 was gutted by fire at the Harper's Heath Hayes site on 21st April, 1966. (Roger F.de Boer)

Ex Birmingham Corporation Transport Daimter type COG, registration number AOG 602 became fleet number 2 in the Harper Brothers fleet. It is shown resplendent in new green and white Harper livery, at Bromford Races, Erdington, Birmingham, in 1947. The side roads around the race course were always lined with buses and coaches of all descriptions. Bromford Race course was subsequently sold for housing development. (K. A. F. Brewin)

because I liked riding on old buses and NAC was a full front [i.e. flush front - not a half-cab] and looked ultra-modern compared to JUE whose body design was virtually the same as the then oldest Tudor Rose coach : FWD 317". Mr. de Boer was not sure whether a defect had developed on NAC, if it were his protestations, however, he was transferred back to JUE for the return journey! Julian Coope confirmed Harper Brothers "did indeed take over Tudor Rose. From September 1960 to July 1961, I travelled on a 'contract' coach from Brownhills to Aldridge Grammar School. [I was 12-13 years old at this time]. Part way through the year, I recall well the change to the older appearance Tudor Rose coaches, with their two tone paintwork and vent fin on the rear of the coach work. I was used to the Leylands run by Harpers and the Tudor Rose coaches were quite a change. The wooden window surrounds and moquette seats still remain in my memory. All were the half cab type. I do recall the rather fine chrome plated leather vent in the centre of the bulk head behind the engine, so perhaps that suggests a winter date for their appearance on my school run". Julian moved schools but still travelled with Harpers "on their normal service double deckers. AEC's and Leylands mostly, I recall".

Harper Passenger Power up Kingstanding Hill

Steve Jackson found the "Harper services were very reliable and however long the queue, everyone seemed to get on. I remember when they had a Leyland Atlantean demonstrator in use in the mid-sixties on the Birmingham route. The bus left Union Street with a standing load on the bottom deck, three to a seat on the top deck and people sat on the stairs as well". Steve recounts a story showing the physical support a Harper passenger gave in a time of crisis. "I also recall everyone getting off an RTL one snowy morning and pushing the bus up Kingstanding hill, to the top!" Summer running, according to Mr. Jackson had its highlights.. "The summer often saw the RT and RTL's running along Aldridge Road with clouds of steam erupting from the radiators, the driver using his windscreen wiper to see his way along. Occasionally we were treated to a more comfortable ride home in one of the then recently delivered Duple Commander bodied Leyland Leopards, and the conductor usually had bell punch tickets that I kept carefully until I got home and could put them between the pages of a book, for safe keeping". Steve endorsed many contributors views "that Harper Bros was a highly thought of firm and the employees seemed to have a deep sense of loyalty to the firm". As I suggested earlier in this book, it is not a text book on the Midland Red, A.T. Hastilow or Harper Brothers, though it may encourage readers to look at other sources of information on the companies or make their own valued contributions from research. Mr. de Boer gave some details about the known disposal of the 5 Tudor Rose coaches in the Harper fleet. There will be more information around somewhere!

Disposal of former Tudor Rose Coaches by Harper Brothers

FWD 317 Dennis Lancet 2OlJ3 Yeates C35F 1947 Withdrawn 1961

NAC 908 162J1OA FC37F 1953 Withdrawn June 1961 Sold to Courtis, Cardiff

TWD 672 Commer Av. III T85AO332 Duple C41F 1956 Withdrawn June, 1961 Sold to Harding and Chinn, Redditch

KUE 373 Dennis Lancet 105J1OB Yeates 39F 1951 HB Fleet No. 18 Withdrawn Jan. 1965

JUE 655 769JE C35F 1950 HB Fleet No. 54 Still in Harpers fleet when gutted by fire on 21st April 1966.

A number of contributors mentioned that in 1967, Harpers introduced a subsidiary company, Tudor Rose Coaches Ltd. Mr. Alan Mills informed me 'subsequently 6 coaches were licensed to Tudor Rose Coaches and the last three of these passed to the Midland Red in September 1974'. The fleet nos. being 53,54 and 56. It would have been interesting to have learned from the Harper management the reasons for creating the subsidiary. Eventually, Harper Brothers, acknowledged as the largest independent operator in the West Midlands Traffic Area, was taken over themselves by the Midland Red on April 18th, 1974. Mr. E. Eccleshall presumed the BMMO "were interested in the services Harper Bros. operated, particularly the 30 minute service between Cannock - Aldridge - Kingstanding to Birmingham City Centre, as well as the Motorway Express between Hednesford -Cannock - Cheslyn Hay and Birmingham city centre. In addition, Harper Bros. held an extensive group of Excursion and Tour Licences with a limited number of works and schools licences", as we have mentioned earlier. Of the

three major players in "Wheels around Sutton". the Midland Red name is seen at Sutton Coldfield, Lichfield and Tamworth on a regular basis, with a garages operating from Cannock and Tamworth. Although there are no Harper Bros. vehicles, the company is still in existence, through regular business meetings. The name of Hastilow and Tudor Rose Coaches has vanished from coach activities, but the removal business is not completely forgotten. The Hastilow family advised me "The Removal business was sold in 1981 to Hingleys of Wolverhampton. They operated from our premises at the Reddicap Trading Estate as Tenant until 1989". I understand from the Company's manager that the Black Country removal vans still carry Hingley Hastilow on the vehicles. Mr. Ted Hastilow informs me "that the Hastilow family is still in business at Reddicap Trading Estate providing maintenance facilities for goods vehicles and dedicated transport as H and S Transport, a title first used at the creation of the firm in the 20s". Thanks to the many people quoted in "Wheels around Sutton", the memories of the BMMO, A.T. Hastilow and Harper Bros. will remain for a long time to come. With the aid of Alan Mills again, of The Omnibus Society. we conclude with the Society's list of bus and coach operators in Sutton Coldfield who have been officially licensed over the years. They are [at 21st June, 1994]:

1. E.J. Walker 'Walkerways' 29 Clarence Gardens 10/49-4/60
2. A.J. Parker 48 Redacre Road 6/66-3/73
3. A.T. & A.E. Hastilow 'Tudor Rose Coaches' 8, The Parade 7/21-6/60
4. T.W. Leadbetter [Falcon Coaches] 37 Holbeche Road 5/58-4/63. Also owned Reddicroft Luxury Coaches (Sutton Coldfield) 6/60-4/63.
5. Maney Coaches, name and address unknown 1958
6. B.S. Russell 4, Hollyfield Road South [BSR Coaches] 3/56-current
7. N.P. Burns [Bob's Taxis] Blackberry Lane 12/67-9/70
8. J. Wheelwright 45 Windyridge Road, Walmley 1954-4/59
9. D.A. Rollason 244 Walmley Road. Minibus only 2/59-4/60
10. C.C. Neville 5 different addresses 3/62-current
11. H.C. Mounteney 194 Reddicap Heath Road 6/53-4/63
12. F.R. Dodsworth 60 Clarendon Road. Minibus only 3/65-5/66
13. H.W. Burns 21 Lyndon Road 6/65-10/73
14. F.S. Faherty 'Tramways' 177 Blackberry Lane 7/70-current
15. A.G. Roberts 30 Little Sutton Road 1/72-9/77
16. I. McCone 49 Harcourt Drive. Minibus only 4/72-10/73
17. W. Mills 278, Highbridge Road, Wylde Green 1/21-finished not known
18. V.L. Johnson, Jockey Road, Sutton Coldfield 1914?-finished not known 18[a]. Johnson Motor Co. Duke Street, Sutton Coldfield 1921-same company as above?
19. E. Taylor [Voyager Midi] 81, Tower Road 8/92-6/93
20. Chasebase Ltd. 2, Manor Road. Minibus only 5/94-current
21. C.R. Clews [Mercury Travel] 94 Turchill Drive 4/95—/93 moved to Armitage, Staffs -/93 and still current
22. Chambers & Co. The Parade Noted in 1912 until ?

So we finish where we came in. Answering some local history questions and raising or leaving others to be answered by later local history researchers. At least we made a start!